D0344944

# 32 Third Graders and One Class Bunny

## Life Lessons from Teaching

*Phillip Done*

A Touchstone Book

Published by Simon & Schuster

New York   London   Toronto   Sydney

TOUCHSTONE
Rockefeller Center
1230 Avenue of the Americas
New York, NY 10020

Names and identifying characteristics of some
individuals in this book have been changed.

Copyright © 2005 by Phillip Done
All rights reserved,
including the right of reproduction
in whole or in part in any form.

TOUCHSTONE and colophon are registered trademarks
of Simon & Schuster, Inc.

For information about special discounts for bulk purchases,
please contact Simon & Schuster Special Sales at 1-800-456-6798
or business@simonandschuster.com.

Designed by Ruth Lee Mui

Manufactured in the United States of America

10  9  8  7  6  5  4  3  2  1

Library of Congress Cataloging-in-Publication Data

Done, Phillip.
    32 third graders and one class bunny: life lessons from teaching / Phillip
Done.
      p. cm.
    "A Touchstone book."
    1. Done, Phillip.  2. Teachers—United States—Biography.  3. Teaching.
    I. Title: Thirty-two third graders and one class bunny.  II. Title.
LA2317.D615A3 2005
371.1'0092—dc22
[B]
                                                          2004065356

ISBN-13: 978-0-7432-7239-1
ISBN-10:    0-7432-7239-0

*To Miss Greco*

# Acknowledgments

My heartfelt thanks to my agent, Janis Donnaud. A writer should be so lucky. To my dear friend Heidi Fisher, I am forever grateful for your unending support and for being there at every step in this journey. At Simon and Schuster, I am indebted to Doris Cooper for editing the book with such care. Special thanks to my family and friends who lived through this whole process with me: Kim Guillet, Piotr Konieczka, Lisa Sturn, Mike Wall, and Dawn Young. And homage to the memory of my dad and grandma; they would have gotten a kick out of all this.

# Contents

# Fall

# Winter

## Spring

# I Am a Teacher

*I read Charlotte's Web* and *Charlie and the Chocolate Factory* every year, and every year when Charlie finds the golden ticket and Charlotte dies, I cry.

I take slivers out of fingers and bad sports out of steal the bacon. I know when a child has gum in his mouth even when he is not chewing. I have sung "Happy Birthday" 657 times.

I hand over scissors with the handles up. My copies of *The Velveteen Rabbit* and *Treasure Island* are falling apart. I can listen to one child talk about his birthday party and another talk about her sleepover and another talk about getting his stomach pumped last night—all at the same time.

I fix staplers that won't staple and zippers that won't zip, and I poke pins in the orange caps of glue bottles that will not pour. I hand out papers and pencils and stickers and envelopes for newly pulled teeth. I know the difference between Austria and Australia.

I plan lessons while shaving, showering, driving, eating, and sleeping. I plan lessons five minutes before the bell rings. I know what time it is when the big hand is on the twelve and the little hand is on the nine. I say the *r* in *library*. I do not say the *w* in *sword*.

I put on Band-Aids and winter coats and school plays. I know they will not understand the difference between *your* and *you're*. I know they will write *to* when it should be *too*. I say "Cover your mouth," after they have coughed on me.

I am a teacher.

I examine new braces and new blisters and holes in mouths where teeth have just fallen out. I can spell *vacuum*. I know the magic word.

I wear four-leaf clovers and dandelions in my shirt pocket that have just been picked with love at recess. I pray for snow days. I pray for Stephen to be absent.

I spend Thanksgiving vacation writing report cards, Christmas vacation cleaning my classroom, and summer vacation taking classes on how to relax. I know the difference between a comma and an apostrophe. I can say "apostrophe."

I buy books about cats and dogs and sharks and volcanoes and horses and dinosaurs. I turn jump ropes and am base in tag. I am glad you can only get chicken pox once.

I correct pencil grips and spelling mistakes and bad manners. I push in chairs all the way, push swings higher, and push sleeves up while children are painting. I can touch the paper cutter.

I own one suit, two pairs of shoes, and eight boxes of graham crackers. I have every teacher mug that Hallmark ever made and every Save the Children tie too. I say, "Use two hands!" when they carry their lunch trays. I say, "Accidents happen," after they did not use two hands.

I wear green on Saint Patrick's Day, red on Valentine's Day, and my bathrobe on Pajama Day. I poke straws into juice boxes and untwist thermos lids that are too tight. I unpeel oranges that are too tight too.

I sign library passes and yearbooks and new casts. I attend soccer games and Little League championships and funerals for guinea pigs. I answer to both "Mom" and "Dad."

I am a teacher.

I hope April Fool's Day is on a Saturday. I blow up balloons that will not blow up. I always blow the whistle too early at recess.

I can borrow and carry very fast. I give them more time to answer six times eight than two times three. I never end a sentence with a preposition. I know what a preposition is.

I draw stars and smiley faces. I say, "Take over," in four square games when I was not looking. Once I forgot eight plus seven.

I know when to say "can" and when to say "may." I have worn green marker, red paint, yellow chalk dust, glue stick, and glitter all on the same day. I hate glitter.

I always begin a sentence with a capital and end it with a period. I always walk in line. I always lose at arm wrestling.

I leave "shuger" and "vilets" misspelled on their valentines. I know all my continents and all my oceans. I tape pages back into books. I can find the end of the new roll of Scotch tape. I call on children whose hands are not raised.

I know that *colonel* is a really hard word to read, and so is *doubt* and so is *gauge*. I know that kids will read *started*, when it says *stared*. I have spelled out *because* and *beautiful* and *friend* six million times.

I am a teacher.

I look both ways before crossing the street. I save balls stuck in basketball hoops. I have given 842 spelling tests and have written "Have a Good Summer!" that many times too.

I collect milk boxes and coffee cans and egg cartons. I know all my times tables. I can type without looking. I know that two pretzels do not equal one Hershey kiss.

I can make a telescope out of a toilet paper roll and a totem pole out of oatmeal boxes. I can make snowflakes out of coffee filters and a space shuttle out of a Pringles can too.

I know my notes because "Every Good Boy Does Fine." I know my directions because I "Never Eat Slimy Worms." I know all my planets because "My Very Elegant Mother Just Sat Upon Nine Pickles." And I can only say my ABCs if I sing them.

I fix watchbands, repair eyeglasses, and search for lost milk money after freeze tag. I know when their fists will make a rock and when they will make scissors.

I know when a child does not understand. I know when a child is not telling the truth. I know when a child was up too late last night. I know when a child needs help finding a friend.

I am a teacher.

# The New Year

# Class List

*I have twenty school photos,* have marched in twenty Halloween parades, and have survived twenty April Fool's Days. I have welcomed 642 third graders into my classroom, and tomorrow I will welcome more.

My principal's name is Cathy Carlson. We have worked together for five years. I like her. Cathy loves children, runs short staff meetings, and brings doughnuts for the teachers after Back to School Night.

This afternoon Cathy dropped my new class list into my mailbox. Last year when she handed out the lists, I sent mine back with a note. It said, "May I have another list, please? I don't like this one."

She sent a note back. It said, "No."

This year I met Dawn in the staff room just after Cathy put the lists into our mailboxes. Dawn teaches third grade right next to me.

"Hey, Dawn, did you get a note from Cathy with your list?" I asked.

"Yeah, why?"

"What did it say?" I asked.

"Have a good year," she answered. "Why, what did yours say?"

*"Phil, no changes!"* I read.

She laughed.

"How many kids did you get?" I asked.

Dawn looked at her list. "Twenty-eight."

"Twenty-eight!" I screamed. "I have thirty-two. How many boys do you have?"

She counted. "Fourteen."

*"Fourteen!"* I yelled. "I have twenty-one!"

"That's not bad," she said.

"Not bad? I have the entire NFL in my room," I whined. "I'll trade you."

*"Phil!"* she screamed.

"Come on!" I begged. "I'll wash your car every week. I'll write all your report cards. I'll do your yard duty for the whole year!"

"Yeah, right. That's what you said last year. Now get out of here." She laughed.

"OK," I said, "but I'm going to go see Cathy about this right now."

I couldn't find Cathy. I didn't expect to. Cathy is never around after she puts the lists in our boxes. Actually, she stays out of sight for the next two weeks and waits until we fall in love with our students and wouldn't dream of giving any of them up. Smart principal.

I walked into my classroom, sat down, and looked more closely at my list. Out of thirty-two children, four were discipline problems, five had limited English, one spoke no English at all, three were in the learning resource program and needed special help, one was a diabetic, two had ADD and had to take Ritalin twice a day, one was severely allergic to bees, one was allergic to peanuts, and one was allergic to eggplant.

I started reading their cumulative folders. These folders contain all the child's report cards, health records, and other important information. Ronny's was three inches thick. Stephen's had five different psychological reports. And Justin's was stamped, "Do not open till 2050."

I stopped reading them.

Hopefully they've changed, I thought. Maybe Stephen went to boot camp over the summer. Maybe Justin moved.

Actually, the class didn't look that bad. I've had worse. One year I had thirty-six kids and twenty-five were boys. That year the women's group at church put cards in my box every Monday morning saying they were praying for me. And once a week they sent me a string bean casserole. If you can believe it, that year three of the girls moved.

You know how the Chinese calendar has the Year of the Rat and the Year of the Snake and the Year of the Monkey? Well, that's sort of how I remember my years too.

My first year was the Year of Samantha. Samantha was a writer. She wrote on her desk, on the bathroom walls, and on Emily. Her favorite thing to do was draw a watch on her wrist with Magic Marker and beg me to ask her what time it was. Once she got mad at me and took a Sharpie to all my art supplies. Now I have twenty boxes of "Fart Supplies."

The Year of Rebecca was special. The first time I called on her, she jumped under her desk and started barking. I told Frank, my very first principal, that I didn't think this was the best placement for her, but he just shrugged. One day he came in to ask me a question, and Rebecca started chewing on his pant leg.

*"What is she doing?"* Frank screamed.

"She's teething," I said.

And so ended the Year of Rebecca.

The Year of Dylan was memorable. Dylan "collected" things—pencils, calculators, car keys, mobile phones, furniture. I had to put padlocks on all the cupboards, my desk, even the rabbit cage. Once I caught him rolling the overhead projector cart out the door. He said it was his, and kept on rolling.

I won't ever forget the Year of Cody. Cody wanted to be in the movies. Literally. He loved videos. Oh, not to watch them— to wrap himself up in them. About once a month I had to untie a hundred yards of videotape from around his arms before he started turning blue.

The Year of Satan was *really* fun. That wasn't his name of course. That's just what I called him. Satan stepped on every snail he saw. He sizzled insects with magnifying glasses. Potato bugs curled up when they saw him coming.

I wonder who this year will be named after. Which one of the thirty-two will be the winner?

# The First Day of School

*This morning,* twenty-one boys and eleven girls walked into their third grade classroom. They sat down, nervous and quiet, trying to figure out their new man teacher with the tie and the glasses who for the first period told them to be thoughtful to others, and use your time wisely, and follow directions, and raise your hands before speaking, and do not touch the paper cutter, and ask to go to the bathroom, and don't whine when you take out your math books, and respect each other's property, and who knows what that means? And don't chew gum at school, and don't exclude others from your games, and walk in the hallways, and don't run up the slide.

Poor kids. I would have left after the first ten minutes.

Actually, I almost did on my first day of third grade. My teacher's name was Mr. Johnson. I cried when I found out I had him. My friends said he was mean. He gave homework. But my mom liked him because he taught kids their times tables and the states, and my mom said that teachers didn't teach kids their times tables and states anymore.

On my first day of third grade, Mr. Johnson lined us all up in front of the chalkboard and walked down the row like a sergeant. He stopped in front of me, bent over, and raised one eyebrow.

"Mr. Done?" he said slowly.

I froze.

"I had your older brother," he said.

I wanted to run out the door but figured that, being a sergeant, he could run faster than I could. So I stayed and learned my times tables and my states.

Now I like the first day of school. I like the newness of it all. The name tags aren't torn. The butcher paper hasn't faded. The pencils don't have teethmarks. The dry erase markers write. The glue bottles pour. The dodgeballs bounce. The watercolor trays are clean. The rug smells like carpet cleaner. And the desks smell like 409.

The boys still line up with the boys, and the girls still line up with the girls. At nine o'clock they still ask me, "When's lunch?" and at ten o'clock, "When's school over?" They still laugh out loud when I read *The Teacher from the Black Lagoon*, even though they heard it in kindergarten and first grade and second grade too. They still forget over the summer how to do 500 minus 199. They still hope the new man teacher likes them.

And I do.

Today was a good day as far as first days of school go. I was lucky. One of Dawn's kids walked home after morning recess. He said he was tired. A girl in Kim's class screamed for three hours straight. A boy in Lisa's class had an accident on the rug. Marion had two criers. And a kid in Mike's room threw up three times before lunch (the custodian finally left the mop).

On the first day of school, kids usually fall in love with their new teacher by first recess. But for me, it takes about a week until they are mine. I always miss the old ones. I look at row two, second seat from the end, and I still see Jesse from last year leaning back on his chair. I look at row one, right on the aisle, and I still see Alexandra with her hair in her mouth. I look at row three, middle seat, and I still see Mark surrounded by pencil sharpener shavings. But Mark is sharpening his pencils, Alexandra is eating her hair, and Jesse is falling over in another classroom this year. They all have their new favorite teachers now.

And that is how it should be.

# Only Thirty-eight Weeks to Go

*Where did my summer go?* I was just beginning to relax. And I was doing so well too. By the end of June I ate a whole piece of watermelon without counting the seeds out loud. By July I cut an apple without asking anybody, "How many quarters make a half?" And in August I even threw away a mayonnaise jar.

Every year I forget what it's like to start all over again. The first week of school comes, and *bam!* I feel like I just jumped into the hamster cage. Actually, the hamster's life is looking pretty darn good right now.

I always forget that third graders at the beginning of the year are *not* the same as third graders at the end of the year. The kids I hugged good-bye in June are not the kids I welcomed last week.

I forget that new third graders can't tell time, they can't read cursive, and they don't know if the holes on the binder paper go on the right or the left.

I forget that they take three hours to write their names on their papers, then another three hours to write five sentences. And the five sentences take up three pieces of paper because they write so big.

I forget that it takes five minutes for them to finish their addition problems (that I planned for them to take an hour for) because they can't remember how to carry, and they just put question marks on all the problems and say they're done.

This week I feel as though all I'm doing is playing chess. First I moved Ronny away from Brian. They were pretending to be kung fu masters. Then I moved him away from Stephen (Ronny discovered that the end of the compass makes an excellent spear). Then I moved him away from Anthony (I had to break up their burping contest). Finally I moved Ronny right beside me. I told him, "One more problem, and king takes pawn outside."

I am already on my ninth seating chart. And just when I have everyone seated in a place I think will work, now they all want to know when they can change seats.

## SEATING CHART

# Names

*I entered teaching* in the *C* years. The boys were all named Christopher. The girls were all named Christine. The hamsters were all named Cookie.

Pretty soon we started reading the classics again, and the room was full of Olivers and Elizabeths and Emmas and Nicholases.

Then came the *J* years. I had four Jacobs, three Jeremys, two Jessicas, and five Jackies in the same room. It made putting names in alphabetical order extremely difficult.

Some trends came and went. Once I had two Blakes, three Ashleys, and a Zack. I thought I was on *One Life to Live*. Another year I felt like I was working at a sweetshop. I had a Candy and a Coco. Then there was the year that I chased Maxes and Trevors and Rexes around all day long. The cafeteria may as well have served Kibbles 'n Bits.

Some years a few names are just too difficult for me to pronounce. These kids quickly receive their new nicknames of Tiger, or Sweetheart, or Trouble.

One year it was May when Sam finally realized that Seung Bin's real name was not Tiger. That was understandable though. Sam thought my first name was Mr.

Sometimes I just don't want to say their names at all. Take the new student who arrived last spring. Guess what his name was?

His name was Phuc.

All day long I would say, "Sit down, Phuc," "Line up for lunch now, Phuc," and, "Phuc, it's time for reading."

I tried making the *u* in his name long. I pretended that I didn't see him raise his hand so I didn't have to call on him. He was my next Tiger.

Some years I swear that all the expectant moms on the PTA get together and say, "OK, girls, what name can we all give our new babies this year?"

One year they decided on Hannah. How do I know this? Because a few years later I had five Hannahs in my classroom, that's why. The only way I could keep them all straight was to number them.

"Hannah Number Three," I said, "would you please answer the question?"

I pointed to Hannah.

"I'm not Hannah Number Three," said Hannah. "I'm Hannah Number Five."

This year I keep calling Brian by his brother's name because I had his brother last year. And I call Joshua "Luke" because Luke was sitting in that seat two months ago.

And forget the attendance sheet. Nobody wants to be called what it says on the attendance sheet anymore. Jenny hates the name Jennifer. Joey hates Joseph. Matthew wants to be called

Matt now, Ronald wants to be called Ronny, and Justin wants to be called the Terminator.

The moms' names are worse. Half of them have different last names from their kids'. Patrick's mom got angry 'cause I wrote "Mrs." and not "Ms." And I'm sorry, but those hyphenated names drive me crazy. They do not fit on my name tags.

My brother Steve is a teacher too. He teaches the older kids. One day, when he and his wife were expecting their first child, they sat around the kitchen table trying to pick out a name. I was with them.

"What about Rachel?" my sister-in-law, Karen, asked.

"No way," said my brother.

"Why?" she asked.

"Because I had a Rachel in my room once," he answered. "She stole everything."

"OK, no Rachel," Karen said. "What about Rebecca?"

I screamed.

"What?" she asked.

"You can't name her Rebecca," I said.

"Why?"

"I had a Rebecca once, and whenever she didn't want to do something, she hid under the desk and barked."

"Oh my. Maybe we should try some boys' names then. I like the name Thomas. Do you like Thomas?" she asked my brother.

Steve looked at her. "Do you want to be penny-locked in the bathroom and pull toilet paper rolls out of the john?" he asked.

Karen made a nervous face.

"How about Jacob?" she suggested.

I pointed to the side of my head.

"See these gray hairs?" I asked.

"Yeah," she answered.

"They're *all* named Jacob. And see this?" I cried, pointing to the bald spot on the top of my head. "I used to have hair there until Nathan showed up."

Karen laughed.

"OK. No Jacob and no Nathan," she said. "But we have to name him *something.*"

"I got it," said my brother. "Let's name him Martin."

"Martin? Why Martin?" she asked.

"Because I have never had a Martin in my class."

"But what if you get a Martin one day in your class and it ends up being the Year of Martin?" she asked.

"No problem." My brother smiled. "We'll just change our son's name."

# Classrooms

*Did you know* that there are only six classrooms in the entire world? It's true. Visit any school, and you will see that all classrooms fall into one of six categories.

Like cars, classrooms have names too. The six models include the Shock, the Chi, the Natural, the Pile, the Hospital, and the Model Home. At my school we have all six of them.

My friend Kim teaches second grade down the hall. Her classroom is the Shock. Every wall, window, door, and cupboard in her room are covered with kids' work, banners, posters, pocket charts, and maps. Not one inch is left uncovered. Not even the ceiling. Of course everything is labeled too—the globe, the paper towel holder, the piano, the bunny.

Dawn teaches in the Chi. She hung mirrors to create balance, plants to soak up noise pollution, and wind chimes to absorb negative energy. Dawn plays soft music during silent reading time. She has an aquarium with goldfish in the back of the room and a small fountain in the corner. She used to burn candles, but once she set off the fire alarm, so she doesn't do that anymore.

Mike's classroom is the Natural. Years ago he threw away all the Rubbermaid, poured everything into baskets, removed the carpet, and pulled out all the fluorescent bulbs. He wears hemp and his kids wear tie-dye. His students macramé their Mother's Day gifts and sit on stumps to eat their carrot sticks.

I am not like Mike or Dawn or Kim. I am a piler. I pile papers on my desk. I pile them on the floor. I pile them on the rabbit cage. I pile on my piles. I have three file cabinets. If you open them, you will see piles. But it is not easy to be a teacher and a piler. Pilers are often misunderstood and made fun of behind their piles—especially by those who work in Hospitals.

Hospitals do not have anything hanging on their walls or ceilings or doors or cupboards. Hospital teachers do not lick their fingers to clean their overhead transparencies. And they do not add extra baking soda and vinegar into the papier-mâché volcano to see how much lava will erupt all over the teacher's desk.

Someday I want to work in the Model Home. It is my fantasy. (Pilers are also dreamers.) My friend Lisa teaches first grade in the Model Home. I love visiting Lisa's classroom. She has fake ficus trees in the corners, plastic runners on her carpet, and guest towels by her sink. Her broom closet has a mirror on it (an upgrade), and her books are all the same color.

Of course, one could be a combination of two classrooms. Mrs. Simon, the science lab teacher, says she is half Natural and half Shock. Marion, my friend who teaches grade two, says she is about seventy-five percent Chi and twenty-five percent Model

Home. And Mrs. Fisher, the music teacher, says she is about one-fifth Shock, and four-fifths Pile. We get along well.

But certain styles are just not compatible with one another. For example, one couldn't be a Pile-Hospital. Well, I guess maybe you could. But your piles would smell like Lysol.

# Mrs. Wilson

*There are some teachers* who make me sick. No matter how hard I try, I will never be like them. Never. Take Mrs. Wilson, for example. I hate her.

Mrs. Wilson's pencil sharpener does not have crayon in it. Mrs. Wilson's smock has no paint on it. The handles of her paintbrushes do not have paint on them either.

Her kids walk in a straight line, do not talk in the hall, do not pick mud off their shoes during story hour, always raise their hands, and never spill paint.

Everything in her room is in alphabetical order—her books, her encyclopedias, her files, her sticker box, even her students. Yes, Derek sits next to Connie, who sits next to Bryce, who sits next to Anna. It's enough to make one vomit. But of course you can't. No one would dare throw up in her classroom. No one has ever thrown up in her classroom.

Mrs. Wilson's celery always turns red when she puts it in food coloring. Her lima bean seeds always sprout in their Ziploc bags, and her salt crystals always grow. I'm convinced that Mrs. Wilson's bunny does not poop.

My compasses point everywhere but north. My batteries are

always dead. My aquarium leaks. And my Venus flytrap is a vegetarian.

Mrs. Wilson changes her bulletin boards diligently each month. Apples make way for pumpkins, which come down for turkeys. When she's putting up snowmen, I'm taking down "What Did You Do This Summer?"

Mrs. Wilson has a box for everything (which she covered herself of course with contact paper)—a box for burlap, a box for felt, a box for orange juice cans, a box for popsicle sticks, a box for rabbit food, a box for straws, a box for yarn. She even has a box for her boxes. (Pilers just cannot comprehend this.)

Her crayons are all in separate containers too. Blue crayons in blue tubs. Red crayons in red tubs. Yellow with yellow. You would never see a green crayon in the blue tub. Never.

My crayons are all in one box—the same box as all my yarn, burlap, felt, straws, orange juice cans, popsicle sticks, and rabbit food.

Once, just for fun, I snuck into her room after work and threw a red crayon in with the yellow ones. But that night I felt so guilty about it that I drove back to school after dinner and put it back.

Mrs. Wilson handwrites each Back to School Night invitation, turns her room into a haunted house for Halloween, dresses up like a pilgrim for Thanksgiving, and has snow shipped in for her winter party. It's even been whispered that the thank-you cards for her Christmas gifts are written, addressed, and stamped *before* she receives the gifts.

Dear Student,

Thank you so much for the beautiful gift. I absolutely love it. I will put it in a very special place, and whenever I look at it, I will think of you.

Love,

Mrs. Wilson

How does she do it, I'd like to know? What is her secret? How is it that her stapler is always full, her glue bottles always pour, her pop-up books still pop up, and her paper clips never hook themselves to each other when you take them out of the box? How, after thirty-five years, does she still have all her checker pieces?

# Teacher School

*One day* while the kids were writing in their journals, Brian shouted out, "How come every teacher always tells me to write in complete sentences?"

"Because that's what we learn to say in Teacher School," I answered.

"What's that?" he asked.

"It's where all teachers learn how to be teachers," I said. "It is sort of like Parent School."

He stared at me.

"You're joking," Brian said.

"No, I'm not," I answered.

"What else do you learn at Teacher School?" Justin joined in.

I paused for a second. "Well," I said in a serious voice, "in the first year you learn how to push a stapler, how to turn a jump rope, and how to cut straight with a paper cutter. You also learn how to blow a whistle, how to put stars on papers, how to pull down a wall map, how to tug on the screen so it goes up on the first try, and how to turn the pencil sharpener really fast. Emptying the sharpener comes later."

"Is this true?" asked Brian.

"Of course it's true," I said. "In year two you learn how to play red rover, how to unjam the copier, and how to change the bulb in the overhead projector. You learn how to make cursive *W*s and *T*s the right way because you forgot. And you practice saying, 'Walk!' until you can say it really loud. I was really good at that."

"We could have guessed that," said Brian.

"What about year three?" asked Justin.

"Well, your junior year is more difficult," I said. "In year three you learn how to pass out papers, how to write in a straight line on the board, how to carve a pumpkin, and how to tell if a child is not telling the truth."

"No way," said Justin.

"Yes way. I studied it very hard. That's why I'm so good at it."

"So is my mom," said Brian.

"See? I told you Teacher School is like Parent School."

"What else?" Justin asked.

"Also in year three," I explained, "you learn how to make a Halloween costume out of a Hefty bag, how to clean a hamster cage, and how to cut a birthday cake into thirty-two pieces with a plastic ruler when a mom sends one in without a knife. Of course year three is when you learn your teacher jokes."

"Teacher jokes?" asked Brian.

"Yes," I said. "Every teacher has to learn at least three jokes in order to graduate."

"That's not true," said Justin.

"Sure it is," I replied.

"Then tell us one," said Brian.

I paused for a second. "OK. Where do all pencils come from?" I asked.

"We know that one," said Justin.

"Well, where from?" I asked.

"Pennsylvania," Justin said.

"That's very good, Justin," I said. "You could be a teacher." He shook his head.

"What about the next year?" asked Brian.

"Oh, the last year is tough."

"Why?" he asked.

"Because in the last year you have to learn to read upside down during storytime, how to lick your fingers before you turn the page, and how to take a messy stack of papers and hit it on the table three times then pat it on the top three times so that it looks nice and neat and the corners are even so now you can staple the stack."

"What else?" asked Justin.

"In the last year," I continued, "you also learn how to open a Band-Aid so that the ends don't stick together before you wrap it around a finger, how to turn a shoe box into a mailbox for valentines, and you have to learn to say all your times tables really fast without looking at the multiplication chart."

"I'm never going to be a teacher," said Justin.

I laughed.

"And," I continued, "seniors must also pass the following classes: Glaring at Children Who Play with Velcro during Story-time, How to Take Away Paper Clips and Rubber Bands, Advanced Juice Box Opening, and How to Make Boys Finish Writing in Their Journals When They Would Rather Talk."

"Mr. Done!" screamed Brian.

"You're fooling us," said Justin.

I laughed. "OK, you two, that's enough. Now get back to work."

Brian smirked. "When did you learn to say *that?*"

"Day one." I winked. "And I was the best in the class."

# You Can Always Expect

*The following are* things you can always expect from kids.

They will always grab the shortest pencil in the pencil box because it is more fun to write with a pencil that is one inch long. But they will always pick the largest pair of scissors from the scissor box because it is more fun to cut with the big scissors.

• • •

If you pass out three Cheerios to each child, but one Cheerio is stuck to another Cheerio so that one child accidentally gets four Cheerios, the child sitting next to the kid who got four Cheerios will scream, "That's not fair!"

• • •

If it is the teacher's birthday, they will guess that you are older than you are. They will guess that you are a hundred.

• • •

When you hand out yardsticks, two boys will begin to sword fight. When they bring you the yardstick in two pieces, one will say, "It just broke."

• • •

When they are sitting in front of the overhead projector and you are tracing their silhouettes with white crayon onto black construction paper for Mother's Day gifts and tell them to sit perfectly still, they will move.

•  •  •

When the prince kisses Snow White, someone will say, "Yuck!" When the prince kisses Cinderella, someone will say, "Yuck!" When it is time for division, they will say, "Yuck," too.

•  •  •

When they are coloring in class, someone will start to hum. While riding in the bus on a field trip, someone will start to sing.

•  •  •

When you point to a paper on the floor and ask, "Whose is this?" no one will answer. When you say, "Pick this up," they will say, "It's not mine."

•  •  •

When they sit on the carpet to hear a story, they will play with their shoelaces and stare at their fingernails as if they have never seen shoelaces and fingernails before.

•  •  •

When you read the story, they will dig for staples in the carpet. When they find a staple, they will hand it to you as if you've been searching for it. When you show everyone the picture in the book, someone will say, "I can't see."

•    •    •

In the middle of a spelling test, someone will ask, "How many words are there?" After you tell them how many words there are, someone will ask, "How many words are there?"

•    •    •

Right before they jump off the jungle gym, they will shout, "Look!" When they are hanging upside down on the monkey bars, they will wave and call your name.

•    •    •

If they eat a red hot candy, they will stick out their tongue and ask you if their tongue is red. When you give them orange slices, they will put the whole slice in their mouth and smile really big so you can see their new orange teeth.

•    •    •

If there is a beanbag chair in the room, someone will dive on it. If there is a beanbag chair in the room tomorrow, he will jump on it again.

•    •    •

When you make green and red paper chains in December, and each child only gets ten strips of paper, they will connect all their chains to make the longest chain ever made.

•   •   •

When you say, "I have eyes behind my head," they will ask you to tell them what is behind you. When you say, "Give me one second," they will count to one.

•   •   •

If there's a swing, they will stand on it. If there's a slide, they will run up it. If there's a fence, they will kick the ball over it.

•   •   •

When there is an exit sign on the ceiling in the hall, they will jump up to hit it.

•   •   •

If the windows are foggy, they will trace their names on them. If your car is dirty, they will write "Clean Me!" on the back window.

•   •   •

When you tell them to go look up a word in a dictionary, they will come back and tell you that the word is not there.

•   •   •

If you walk toward them with mistletoe, they will run. When they make valentines, they will sign them "From." When they eat their hollow chocolate Easter bunnies, they will always bite the ears off first.

•  •  •

They will always leave the last *e* out of *sincerely* and the *d* out of *Wednesday*. They will spell *sure* with an *h,* and the second letter in *improve* will be an *n.*

•  •  •

When you give them a measuring tape, they will pull it out all the way so that it won't go back in again. When they lean against the broom closet so you can measure their heights, they will stand on tiptoe.

•  •  •

When you drive behind the school bus on the way home, they will wave to you and make faces. If you wave and make faces too, they will laugh and keep waving and making faces as long as you drive behind the bus.

•  •  •

When you get to school the next morning, they will run up to you and say they saw you driving behind the school bus yesterday as if you didn't know it was you behind them.

•  •  •

They will say "cinnamon" when it says "synonym." They will write as small as they can, and when you say, "It's too small. I can't read it," they will read it out loud to you.

•  •  •

If you act out *Peter and the Wolf,* all the boys will want to be Peter. If you act out *Hansel and Gretel,* all the girls will want to be Gretel. If you act out *Snow White and the Seven Dwarfs,* the whole class will want to be Dopey.

• • •

If there is both an electric pencil sharpener and a manual one in the room, they will always choose the electric sharpener, then grind the pencil down so far that they have to sharpen another one.

• • •

On the last day of school, one of the kids will cry. On the last day of school, so will I.

# Teacher Moments

*There are certain moments* in teaching that I call Teacher Moments. These are the special moments that make it all worthwhile. They are golden. They are few. They come unannounced. And you have to listen very closely, or you might miss them.

When Cameron pulled his mother into the classroom after school, picked up *The Cat in the Hat,* and shouted, "Look, Mom, I can read!"—that was a Teacher Moment.

When I closed *Treasure Island,* and they all screamed, "Don't stop!"—that was a Teacher Moment too.

When Jack, whom I had suspended three times during the year, would not let go of me on the last day of school, that was a Teacher Moment.

When Sofia, who a year before could not speak one word of English, stood in front of the whole school and recited "Stopping by Woods on a Snowy Evening"; when I received a letter from Victor saying that he is in college now and wants to be a teacher just like me; and when James asked me if *Charlotte's Web* is a true story—those were all Teacher Moments.

Unfortunately, when the moments come, I usually don't have a pencil handy, or I say I'll write it down later but forget, or

I simply wasn't listening closely enough that day and missed the moment completely.

But one day, not too long ago, I didn't miss it. I was sitting with my students in the corner of the classroom.

"Boys and girls," I said, "do you know what the person is called who writes a book?"

"An author," said Emily.

"That's right, Emily. And does anyone know what the person is called who puts the whole book together?"

"A book maker?" Peter answered.

"That's close, Peter. A person who makes books is also called a publisher."

I held up *Happiness Is* by Charles Schulz.

"See this book," I said. "It is made, or printed, by a publisher. Charles Schulz wrote the book and illustrated it. Then he sent it to a publisher. The publisher is the one who puts it all together into an actual book."

I continued, "But you cannot always find any book you want in a bookstore. Sometimes the publisher stops printing the book. Then we say that the book is not in print anymore."

Andrew raised his hand.

"Yes, Andrew?" I asked.

He had a worried look on his face.

"But, Mr. Done," he asked, "can you get it in cursive?"

That one I remembered to write down.

# The Laminating Machine

*I used to laminate everything,* absolutely everything—posters, prints, bookmarks, birthday certificates, awards, library passes, name tags, file folders, book jackets, real estate calendars. You name it, I laminated it. They called me the laminating king.

It got pretty bad. Once Cathy sent me a note with a question. Attached was a sticky note. It said, "Please just answer question. Do not laminate."

But now I won't go near the machine. Not even close.

You see, one night I was in the staff room laminating my kids' art for Back to School Night. It was late.

Now, you know what a laminating machine looks like of course. It's about three feet wide and sits on a table. It has two big rolls of plastic. You put whatever it is you want to laminate in on one side. The paper rolls through the two big rolls of laminating plastic. The plastic is hot and adheres to the paper. And your paper comes out on the other side all nicely laminated. It's great.

So there I was, carefully guiding each piece of artwork into the laminator, humming along, when all of a sudden, I felt this *tug!* I looked down. My tie was caught in the machine!

Immediately, I pulled back, but the tie was stuck. I tugged again. Still nothing. I jerked a third time. No luck. Meanwhile, I was still rolling into the machine. Oh my God, I thought. I am going to die!

I could see the headlines: "Teacher Flattened in Laminating Machine," "Teacher Suffocates to Death in Hot Plastic," "Teacher Becomes Art Project," "J. C. Penney Recalls One Million Ties."

I slammed off the switch.

I kept rolling.

"Crap!" I screamed.

It was the heat button.

I pushed another button.

I started rolling faster.

"Nooooo!" I yelled.

I reached under the table and fumbled for the cord. I found it. Thank God!

I yanked it as hard as I could.

Suddenly everything stopped.

I sighed, closed my eyes, and rested my chin on the edge of the table. I didn't move for about ten seconds. My head was about five inches away from the roller.

Finally I lifted my head and looked around the room.

How the hell am I going to get out of this thing? I thought to myself. I couldn't undo my tie. The skinny part in the back had gone through too.

Then I spotted some scissors on the counter. I tried to reach them but they were too far away.

Damn! What was I going to do?

"Helloooooo," I said softly. "Hellooooo."

Nobody answered.

Oh my God, I thought. If I don't get out of here, the other teachers will find me here in the morning.

I yelled louder.

*"Heeelp! Heeeeelp!"* I screamed.

Finally, after about ten minutes of my screaming at the top of my lungs, Marion walked into the room. She covered her mouth.

"Don't laugh," I said. "Get me out of this thing!"

"How did you . . . ? " she asked.

"Never mind! Just get me out of this," I said. "Grab those scissors over there and cut the tie."

"Cut it?"

"Cut it!" I screamed.

"But it's a nice tie," she said.

"I don't care about the stupid tie," I yelled. "Just get me out of here! And stop laughing! It's not funny."

Marion cut the tie and I was saved. That night I made her swear to not tell a soul. But Marion is not good at keeping secrets. For weeks afterward, strangers would pass me in the supermarket, at the gas station—everywhere—point to my tie, and start cracking up.

I called my dad and told him the whole story. He couldn't stop laughing either. Until I told him it was his tie.

# Back to School Night

*The day before Back to School Night,* Kim and I were decorating the cafeteria. Each teacher had to put up something their students had made. My kids drew self-portraits but Katie insisted on drawing a bear. So, I teach thirty-one kids and one koala. Kim's first graders wrote sentences about what their parents do while they are at school.

Austin wrote, "When I'm at school, my mommy drops my sister off then goes home and watches TV."

Carlota wrote, "When I'm at school, my daddy goes somewhere, but I don't know where."

Debbie wrote, "When I'm at school, my mom goes to the supermarket and buys Pepsi Light."

And Lambert wrote, "When I'm at school, my dad builds tables." (Lambert's dad works in a bank.)

As Kim and I hung up the kids' work, I thought back to my very first Back to School Night. I remember when I walked into my classroom that first September and announced, "Boys and girls, today we will not be doing math."

Everyone cheered.

"Try not to be too upset," I said.

"Why aren't we doing math today?" Samantha asked.

"Because we are going to do art all day long, that's why," I answered. "Back to School Night is tonight and look at those bulletin boards."

"What bulletin boards?" asked Richard.

"Just my point," I said. "Now here's some paper. Everyone draw pictures of yourselves. And draw them really big because I have to fill up all those boards."

After an hour, the bell rang for recess. The kids went outside. I ran into the principal in the hall.

"Hey, Frank, how long am I supposed to talk to my parents tonight?" I asked.

"One hour," he replied.

"What!" I screamed. "I can't talk for an hour! What am I going to talk about for an hour?"

"Oh, you'll do fine. Just make a plan," he said. And he walked away.

A plan? Yes, a plan. That was a good idea.

So I began to make a plan: First I'll greet them (that will take five seconds). Then I'll welcome them all (five more seconds). Then I'll introduce myself (ten seconds). Great, I thought. I have filled twenty seconds.

I was in trouble.

I went to see Mike. Mike had been teaching for years. Surely he'd have some good ideas.

"Hi, Mike," I said. "What are you doing for Back to School Night?"

"Oh, we're playing a game," he said.

*"A game?"* I screamed. "What sort of game?"

"Oh, one where the parents have to mix and mingle and find out information about each other," he explained. "It's a good ice-breaker."

"I don't have time to break any ice!" I shouted. "My kids are doing art!"

I left Mike and went to Lisa's room.

"Hi, Lisa. What are you doing for Back to School Night?" I asked.

"Oh, I'm doing a slide show." She smiled.

*"A slide show?"* I yelled.

"Yep. I love doing a slide show. I just show the slides and talk. That way I don't have to look at the parents. And they don't look at me because they're looking at the slides."

"Great idea!" I said. "I'll do a slide show too. What kind of slides do you show?" I asked.

"Well," she explained, "I took pictures over the last two weeks of all the kids doing different activities and had them made into slides."

"Can I use them?" I asked.

"They're of my kids," Lisa said.

I grinned. "Do you think the parents would notice?"

"Out!" she screamed, pointing to the door.

I went to see Marion. She was greasing a cookie sheet.

"Hi, Marion. I need some ideas for Back to School Night. What are you doing for tonight?" I asked.

I looked at the cookie sheet and began shaking my head.

"Don't tell me," I said slowly.

"What?" she asked.

"You're *not*," I cried.

"Not what?" she asked.

"Tell me you're *not* making cookies," I whined.

She nodded. "We're making them after lunch, and then we're decorating them. And they wrote their own cookie poems. Want to see them?"

"No! I do not want to see their cookie poems!" I screamed. "I don't have time to decorate cookies and write cookie poems!"

"Don't worry," Marion said. "I'm sure whatever you do will be wonderful."

The bell rang. I walked back to my room. On my way, I ran into Frank again.

"Oh, Phil," he said, "don't forget. Tonight you also need to tell your parents about your goals and expectations for the year."

"Goals? What goals?"

"Your goals for the year."

"Goals for the year?" I screamed. "My goal is to get through tonight!"

I walked into my classroom and opened the closet.

"Why are you pulling out Monopoly?" Samantha asked.

"I thought it would be a good icebreaker."

Frank popped his head in.

"Hey, I'm going to the store after school. Can I get you anything?" he asked.

"Yeah, can you pick me up a couple of bags of Oreos? I

thought I should serve some cookies. No, wait! Get Fig Newtons. They take longer to chew."

"No problem," he said. "Fig Newtons comin' right up."

At three thirty the kids left and I began to clean the room. I put up the artwork, straightened my piles, scraped glue off the desks, threw everything that was on my desk into my desk, changed the newspaper in the rabbit cage, borrowed a couple of sunflowers from the vase in the office, dusted the globes, hid my correcting basket, put the sunflowers in a coffee can, and pulled out a bunch of books on space so parents would think I'm teaching it.

At seven o'clock I opened the door. A man walked in, shook my hand, and said hello. He did not say his child's name. I did not want to ask, "Who are you?" So I took a guess.

"You must be Rodney's dad," I said hesitantly.

"Yes." He smiled.

Why do all parents assume that I will know exactly who they are at Back to School Night when I have never seen them before? I just *love* playing Guess the Parent.

Next a mom came up to me and shook my hand.

"Chip is just loving this class," she said.

I smiled really big.

Who is Chip? I thought.

"He talks about school every day," she said.

I continued to smile and shake her hand.

Who the *hell* is Chip?

"How's he doing in class?" she asked.

"Uh," I said, "well . . . he's . . ."

Maybe she's in the wrong room, I thought.

Then it hit me.

"Oh, *Charles!*" I screamed. "Yes, yes. Of course. Charles! You're Charles's mom! Charles is doing great. I mean Chip. Chip is doing great. Just great."

I gave a big sigh. Guess the Child is fun to play too.

Soon the rest of the parents streamed in. They walked around the room admiring the bulletin boards and the space books. Finally I asked everyone to please take their seats and began my presentation.

"Good evening," I said. "I'd like to welcome you all to Back to School Night. My name is Mr. Done. I'm so happy you all came tonight."

I glanced down at my watch. Fifty-nine minutes and forty seconds to go. I looked up.

"Uh . . . would anyone like a cookie?"

# Tired

*I am so glad* I am not a first-year teacher anymore. The first year is definitely the hardest. My first year I would teach all day, stay at work till seven, go home, eat, and return to school till ten or eleven o'clock at night just to be ready for the following day. I was exhausted. Then the next day I'd do it all over again. My only friend was Al, the night custodian. He sang Russian folk songs while I laminated.

One day I decided I needed a break. Plus the laminator was broken. So I left school early. On my way home, I stopped by some new model homes. I love visiting model homes. The tables are not covered with stickers. The toilet seats are clean. The garbage cans are empty. But the best part is that the kids who live there are just make believe.

I walked inside the first model and was greeted by a very nice real estate agent named Mary. She did not give me her business card. Somehow she realized that I could not afford the pillow on the couch. Maybe it was the paint on my shoes that gave me away. Or maybe it was the glitter glue I was wearing on my slacks.

I walked into the kitchen and opened the fridge. I don't know why I did this. Force of habit, I guess. The fridge was empty, so I went upstairs. I walked straight into the bathroom.

There was no door. So I didn't use it. Now I know why they keep the doors off.

Then I walked into the master bedroom. There in the center of the room was a queen-size bed with about seventeen pillows and some sort of canopy over it. Nobody else was upstairs. So I sat down on the bed. It was very comfortable.

"Hellooooo!" said a voice.

I opened my eyes. Mary stood over me smiling.

"Time to wake up, sunshine," she sang.

I popped up. The pillow was covered with drool.

"Uh . . ." I laughed. "Looks like I fell asleep."

"You sure did, sweetie."

I turned over the pillow, ran down the stairs, and out the front door. Now when I visit model homes, I stay downstairs.

# The Potluck

*In the beginning* of each school year, we have grade level potlucks. It's a chance for the parents to mingle with their child's teacher. For most teachers, the potluck is right up there with staff meetings and cafeteria duty and writing report cards. This year Dawn and I went together.

The one good thing about the potluck, however, is the food. All the moms try to outdo each other. And there are always tons of leftovers. So I bring Tupperware. Dawn hates when I do this.

After putting on our name tags, Dawn and I sat at one of the tables with a group of Japanese moms. They stared at my pile of sushi and giggled as I sat down.

"I love sushi." I smiled.

They giggled some more.

Though most of the moms could not speak English very well, Dawn and I tried our best to communicate with them. We talked about the sushi and school and Japan. Dawn asked the moms if they missed Japan. They said yes.

About halfway through dinner, Dawn smiled at the mom sitting directly across from her, pointed to herself, and said, "I miss Canada." (Dawn is Canadian.)

The mom's eyes grew very big. She said something to the

other moms in Japanese. Soon all the moms were smiling and clapping and speaking very fast. One of them patted Dawn on the head.

"Congratulations," she said.

Neither Dawn nor I understood what the fuss what about. Then the mom who was patting Dawn pretended to place a crown on Dawn's head.

"You Miss Canada," she said. "You Miss Canada."

Dawn gasped. "No, no, no! I am not Miss Canada!"

The moms looked confused.

"I miss Canada. Not *Miss* Canada," Dawn tried to explain. "You miss Japan. I miss Canada. I am not Miss Canada."

One of the moms finally got it and explained it to the others. Then everyone laughed. For the next ten minutes, one mom would point to Dawn and say, "You no Miss Canada. You miss Canada," and laugh until another one would take over and do the same. Dawn tried her best to not look embarrassed, but I knew she was.

After a couple more plates of sushi, we said good-bye to our new Japanese friends and walked out to the parking lot. I walked with Dawn to her car. After she unlocked the door, I grabbed the handle and opened the door for her.

"What are you doing that for?" she asked.

"'Cause you're Miss Canada." I smiled.

"Shut up."

# Picture Day

*I like Picture Day.* It is the one day of the year when T-shirts are traded for button-downs, sweatpants are replaced with pants without holes, and the room is full of new haircuts and hairbows.

This year, as the kids took their seats, I scanned the room. Peter had a new crew cut. Amanda's hair was freshly curled. Stephen's hair was spiked. Carlos's hair wouldn't move because it had so much gel in it. Ronny wore a white polo shirt that I'm sure his mother fought to get on him. Justin wore new jeans. Melissa wore a T-shirt with a large sequined skull and crossbones. (Did her mother know it was Picture Day?) Erika wore a new pink headband. And Nicole had a new hairdo.

"Nicole, how many clips do you have in your hair?" I asked.

"Twenty!" she said proudly.

She looked like a power plant.

Then I looked at Andrew.

"Andrew!" I screamed. "What happened to your hair?"

"I cut it."

"I can see that," I said. "But why?"

"For Picture Day."

"What did you use?"

"My scissors."

"Your kid scissors?"

"Uh-huh."

"What did your mom say?"

"She got mad."

"Stephen, do you have any more of that gel?" I asked.

"Yeah," he replied.

"May I use some, please? I have to try to fix Andrew's hair."

"It won't work," said Andrew.

"Why?" I asked.

"My mom already tried."

Two recesses, one lunch, one PE class, and five games of capture the flag later, it was time for my class to line up for our photos.

Ronny's white shirt had had spaghetti for lunch. Justin's jeans had played three games of soccer (it rained last night). Carlos's hair was smooshed. Amanda had lost her curls, Stephen had lost his spike, and Nicole had lost thirteen hair clips.

The photographer asked me to place the kids in four rows, tallest in the back, shortest in the front.

"Melissa, do you have a sweater, honey?" I asked.

"No," she answered.

"Then why don't you stand in the second row right behind Isabel."

"But I'm the shortest."

"You grew at lunch," I said. "Go stand behind Isabel."

I looked at Ronny.

"Ronny, you can't stand in the front row either. It looks like you were shot. Go stand in the back."

Kenny was trying to wipe the grass stains off his jeans.

"Kenny, you look like a Tide commercial. Go stand next to Ronny."

Then I took my place in the back row.

"Ready?" the photographer asked.

I sighed. "Yes," I said.

"OK, here we go, everyone," the photographer said.

"Justin, put your hands down," I said through my teeth.

"Now, on the count of three, everyone say cheese," said the photographer.

"Aaron, take your hands off Carlos's hair!" I screamed.

"One," the photographer began to count.

"Peter, turn around!" I yelled.

"Two," he continued.

"Justin, did you take out your tooth guard?"

"Three!" he shouted.

*"Cheese!"* We all smiled.

The class photos arrived five weeks later. Peter was a blur. Emily's eyes were closed. Anthony was looking at Carlos. Carlos was making bunny ears over Stephen. I looked like I was saying a bad word. And Justin looked like he had a hockey puck in his mouth.

Out of the whole class, only one of us looked halfway decent—Andrew.

# How Many Hats Do I Wear?

*I am a doctor.* I put my hand on foreheads that are too hot to do math today.

I am a dentist. I examine braces that are too tight to do math today too.

I am a taxi service. I make sure all seatbelts are buckled on the way to the pumpkin patch, the firehouse, the zoo, the airport, the hospital, and the farm to see the new baby pigs.

I am an actor. Learning your times tables can be fun.

I am a mom. I clean up throw-up.

I am a detective. I know whose paper it is when there is no name on it.

I am a decorator. I wallpaper in yellow butcher paper. I accent with green beanbag.

I am a repairman. I know how to put cardboard under a desk leg so it won't wobble. I can remove the thirteen staples that have just turned into one after being pounded in the stapler. I mend bruised feelings and bicycle chains and broken shoelaces.

I am a librarian. I know exactly where the book with the great white shark on the cover is in the library.

I am a coatrack. I hold sweaters so you can slide, lunch money so you can slide, and glasses so you can slide some more.

I am an electrician. I can make circuits that are parallel and circuits in series if I study the drawing in the teacher's manual at recess right before the kids come in.

I am an athlete. I can run to the bathroom and back in two minutes.

I am a mailman. I send home important newsletters about school photos so that your mom can call me and ask why she never heard about Picture Day.

I am a musician. I can play both parts to "Heart and Soul."

I am a mathematician. I know that 32 kids – Brian = easier day.

I am a businessman. I loan money for lunch at a reasonable interest rate.

# Class Pet

*We have a class bunny.* Her full name is Penelope Precious Buttercup III. I did not name her. The kids voted.

The other day I was filling up Penelope's water bottle—because the rabbit monitors, who begged me to get a bunny and promised to take care of her, did not see that the water bottle was empty.

Anyway, I was attaching the water bottle to Penel's cage, when I noticed that she wasn't eating her food. I opened her cage, picked her up, and began to search for why a perfectly healthy-looking bunny wasn't eating. I poked and prodded, then opened her mouth.

"Aah!" I screamed. Her teeth were about an inch long and curved. She couldn't even close her mouth. After school, I drove Penel to the vet.

"What seems to be the problem?" the vet asked.

"Something is wrong with my bunny," I said. "She won't eat. I think something's wrong with her teeth."

"Let's have a look," he said.

He opened Penel's mouth and examined her teeth.

"Her teeth are maloccluded," he said matter-of-factly.

"They're what?" I asked.

"Maloccluded," he repeated.

"What the hell is that?"

"She has buckteeth," he answered.

"So, what do I do—take her to the orthodontist and get bunny braces?"

"No, you cut them."

"Cut them?" I screamed.

"Yes. It's no problem," he replied.

"And how am I supposed to do that?"

"You just get some wire cutters and cut them to the right length."

"You're kidding?"

"No. I'm serious."

"So, you're telling me that all I have to do is get some wire cutters and open her mouth and go snip snip, and that's it?" I asked.

"That's it," he said.

Scenes from *Fatal Attraction* popped into my head.

"I can't do that," I said. "Can you do it, please?"

He did. And fifteen minutes later, Penel could eat again.

Oh, I'm *so* glad I bought a class pet. I'm *so* glad I listened to all my friends and got a cute little bunny rabbit.

"Bunnies are so easy," they all told me. "No work at all. Nothin' to it. The kids will love it."

Ha! No trouble at all. Nothing to it. Yeah, right!

Excuse me, everyone! You all forgot to mention that I will have to take the cute little bunny to the vet once a month and have her teeth sawed off. You also neglected to tell me that it will cost seventy-five dollars a pop so Penel can chew her carrots!

So much for an easy class pet! Guess what? Now the class wants a snake! I said no way. I'd probably have to cut its teeth once a month too.

# Officer Joe's Visit

*The last week in September* is always a special week at our school. It is Bicycle Safety Week. And every year during Bicycle Safety Week, Officer Joe comes for a visit.

Officer Joe's visit is always the same. He parks his car on the blacktop. Then all the first, second, and third graders walk outside in single file lines and sit down in rows on the cement. Then Officer Joe talks about how to ride a bicycle, turns on the siren, and one lucky child gets to wear Officer Joe's hat and ride in the police car around the blacktop.

But this year there was a surprise. After Officer Joe parked his car and talked about how to ride a bicycle and turned on the siren, he opened his back car door, and out jumped Max. Max is a German shepherd. Max helps Officer Joe.

Then Officer Joe wrapped a thick towel around his arm. After he finished taping the towel, he started to run away from Max. When Officer Joe was about thirty feet away from Max, Officer Joe blew his whistle.

Immediately Max ran toward Officer Joe. Officer Joe put down his arm. Max jumped, grabbed the towel, and stopped Officer Joe. Officer Joe could not run anymore. The kids stood and cheered, and all the teachers screamed, "Sit down!"

Then Officer Joe announced, "I need a volunteer."

Immediately all the kids raised their hands and screamed, "Me! Me! Me!" and all the teachers screamed, "Sit down!" again.

But Officer Joe said, "I need a teacher volunteer."

Matthew began chanting, "Mr. Done! Mr. Done!"

I glared at him. "Matthew!" I yelled. "Be quiet!"

He continued.

Soon the rest of the class joined him. "Mr. Done! Mr. Done!" they chanted loudly.

Officer Joe smiled, walked over to me, grabbed my arm, and escorted me out to the field. Everyone started laughing. Matthew pointed at me. I looked out at the audience and smiled nervously. Then Officer Joe began to wrap the thick towel around my arm.

"What are you doing?" I asked.

"Just run away like I did," he said. "Put your arm down behind you. Max will grab your arm."

"What?" I asked.

"It won't hurt at all," continued Officer Joe. "Max is trained to hold you, not to bite. Just put your arm down. He'll grab the pad. It's perfectly safe."

I looked down at Max.

"Nice doggie." I smiled.

Max panted.

"Are you ready?" asked Officer Joe.

"No," I said.

"Don't worry," said Officer Joe. "Just run when I say to. Got it?"

"Got it," I answered nervously.

He continued, "And when you hear the whistle, put your arm down behind you. OK?"

I nodded. "OK," I said.

"Ready?" he asked.

I took a deep breath. "Ready."

Then Officer Joe yelled, "Run!"

I started running. The kids started screaming. After about three seconds, I turned around. Officer Joe was still holding Max. This wasn't too bad, I thought.

Then Officer Joe blew his whistle.

I ran faster.

All of a sudden, I felt a tug on my pant leg.

*Wham!* I was flat on the grass. (Apparently Max does not know the difference between a leg and an arm.)

"Let go!" I screamed. "Max, *let go!*"

The children roared. Clearly they thought that this was all part of the show. Well, apparently Max is also a big show-off. He began dragging me across the field by my pant leg. Then my pants began to come off. I held on for dear life.

Officer Joe finally arrived and pulled Max off.

"I'm so sorry," he said. "I'm so sorry."

I could not move. "What happened?" I asked, still flat on my back.

"You forgot to put your arm down. Why didn't you put your arm down?" he asked.

"How am I supposed to put my arm down when I'm being chased by Cujo?" I yelled.

"I'm so sorry," he repeated. "Really."

I could see he felt really bad.

Officer Joe helped me up. Everyone applauded. My kids ran up to me.

"Mr. Done, do it again! Do it again!" they screamed.

"No, no," I said, "Max has to go now."

"Why?" they whined.

"Because Max is late for his appointment," I answered.

"Where does he have to go?" asked Matthew.

"To Doggie School," I said. "For the next twelve years!"

# Frog and Toad

*My students* are supposed to read with their parents every night, and every night their parents are supposed to sign their kid's reading log.

Ronny's reading log is never signed. I asked him if his mother helps him at home. He said no.

Ronny needs the help. He struggles in reading.

One Friday I sent another letter home to Ronny's mom explaining the importance of reading with your child. I included another reading log and an article from *The Reading Teacher*. I also sent home a big manila envelope with *Curious George* and *Where the Wild Things Are* and *Frog and Toad*.

On Monday morning Ronny brought back the envelope.

"So, Ronny, did you read with your mom this weekend?" I asked.

He looked down. "No," he said. "She was busy."

I gave a big sigh and shook my head. Too busy? Too busy for her own kid? I was tired of these families that don't value education.

For the next two weeks I continued to send home books in the manila envelope. They continued to come back unread. Ronny continued to give excuses.

Finally I called Ronny's mom in for a conference. Surely this would help. Mrs. Hanson came in the following day. She was very pleasant. She thanked me many times for working so hard with Ronny. Again I explained the importance of reading every day. I gave her a stack of flash cards with sight words, and I copied another article from *The Reading Teacher*. I also lent her two books on reading strategies for children with reading difficulties. She thanked me again.

A couple of days later, I was listening to Ronny read and asked, "Hey Ronny, how's the reading going at home?"

He stopped and put his head down. He did not answer.

"Your mom is reading with you now, right?"

He shook his head. "No," he said softly. "She's busy. She's got things to do."

"Things to do?" I said.

"Yeah," said Ronny, "she's taking night classes now. She gets home from work and makes dinner really fast, then goes out, and when she comes home, I'm in bed. She wants to read with me, but she doesn't have time."

I was mad.

Here Ronny's mom is out doing who-knows-what, and her son sits at home neglected. Some of these parents! So wrapped up in their own lives that they don't even have time for their kids.

On Monday night I was at home mowing the lawn when I remembered I was supposed to be at school helping Dawn with registration for adult education. I raced to school and ran into the building. Dawn was with a student.

"Dawn, sorry I'm late," I said.

"No problem," she said. "We're almost finished."

I sat down and started taking off my jacket.

"Hello, Mr. Done," I heard someone say.

I looked up. It was Ronny's mom.

"Uh . . . hello, Mrs. Hanson," I said, surprised.

Dawn handed her the registration form.

"Good to see you, Mrs. Hanson," Dawn said. "Glad to have you back."

Mrs. Hanson took the form and looked at it. Then she began rummaging through her purse.

"Oh my goodness. I must have left my glasses at home. Would you mind helping me fill this out, please?" she asked Dawn.

"Of course not." Dawn smiled.

Mrs. Hanson shook her head. "Sometimes I'm so absent-minded. I can't believe I forgot my glasses." She laughed.

Dawn helped her with the form and pointed her to the classroom down the hall.

"Oh, thank you so much," she said. "Good-bye."

"Good-bye." I smiled.

And she walked down the hall.

After she left, I leaned over to Dawn. "You know who that was?" I asked. "That's Ronny's mom. She won't help her son but will come here and take a pottery class."

Dawn stared at me.

"Phil," she said. "Do you know which class Ronny's mom is taking tonight?"

"No," I said.

She paused. "Beginning reading," Dawn said.

I stared at her.

"Mrs. Hanson cannot read," she said. "In fact, every one of the parents who signed up for that class forgot their glasses tonight."

I did not move.

How many other parents like Mrs. Hanson have I handed helpful articles to? To how many other parents who could not read have I sent school newsletters and field trip notes? How many other parents have I judged so unfairly?

How many other Ronnys have I forced to make excuses? How many other Ronnys have I sighed deeply at and embarrassed? How could I call myself a reading teacher? How could I call myself a teacher at all? I felt so ashamed.

A few days later I asked Mrs. Hanson to come in for another conference, and I apologized.

"Please don't apologize, Mr. Done," said Mrs. Hanson. "I want to thank you."

I looked up at her. Mrs. Hanson pulled a big manila envelope out of her purse.

Then she said, "Mr. Done, last night I read *Frog and Toad*— with a little help from Ronny, but last night I read *Frog and Toad!*"

She laughed.

"I never thought I'd learn to read," Mrs. Hanson continued.

"Not in a million years. And you helped me, Mr. Done. You helped me. I'm grateful that you sent all those books home every night with Ronny. Thank you, Mr. Done. You helped me learn to read."

Some days, when everyone is gone, you close the door and cry. This was one of those days.

# Fall

# The Pie-Eating Contest

*Every October* the PTA at my school puts on a big carnival—snow cones, cotton candy, clowns—the works. It's the big fund-raiser of the year.

All the teachers work at the carnival. This year I called out numbers in the cake walk and sold pumpkins in the pumpkin patch behind the library. It beat last year, though. Last year I sat in the dunking booth.

My school carnival always reminds me of the school carnivals that we used to have when I was a kid—especially the famous one when I was in third grade.

It was the end of the day. The final event was about to take place, the event that every child looked forward to—the pie-eating contest. The contest was divided into three categories—kindergarten and first graders together, second and third graders in another group, and fourth and fifth in another.

My two brothers, Carl and Steve, and I all signed up. Carl was in the older kids' group, I was in the middle, and Stevie was with the little ones.

At three o'clock the cafeteria tables were rolled outside and stretched across the blacktop in a line. More than a hundred kids sat on the benches. The pies were laid out on the tables. A local restaurant donated them.

Hundreds of parents and kids surrounded the benches. The fourth and fifth graders sat at one end of the tables. The second and third graders sat in the center, and the little kids at the other end. My mom stood in the back of the crowd.

The rules:

Eat everything in the pie tin.
Don't use your hands.
Stop if you're feeling sick.

Mr. Mason, the principal, held up his megaphone and called out, "Are you ready?"

The kids screamed, "Yeah!"

"OK, everyone," he announced, "On your marks. Get set. *Go!*"

And we were off! Like rockets, we threw our faces into over a hundred tins of apple, blueberry, and cherry filling. The crowd cheered.

In just five minutes the older kids were almost finished. The crowd rushed over to that end of the tables, where over fifty children raced to finish their pies. Two boys in the center of the group were half a pie ahead of the rest. They were neck and neck. The crowd started chanting, "Go! Go! Go!" Mr. Mason stood right beside the two boys watching closely. He leaned over them.

"And the winner is . . . ," he said.

Carl popped up first.

"Carl Done!" he yelled.

The crowd applauded.

Carl beamed. And my mom witnessed ten years of saying, "Slow down," "Chew your food," and "Take smaller bites," disappear in front of her eyes.

Immediately the crowd ran over to the second and third graders. Harold Parks had won three years in a row and was the hands-down favorite.

The crowd began chanting, "Harold! Harold! Harold!"

Then someone screamed, "Hey! Look at that boy!"

Everyone looked.

At the corner of the table sat a little boy, his face buried in blueberry. Suddenly he came up for air.

"Hi, Mom!" I yelled.

She gave half a smile. Then I threw my head back down into the blueberries and surged to the finish.

Mr. Mason shouted, "Phillip Done is the winner!"

The crowd cheered again. Then, like a swarm of bees, everyone ran over to the little kids. News spread rapidly that there was a third Done boy in the little kids' group. If Steve Done won, this would be a sweep. Never before in the history of the pie-eating contest had one family won in all three categories. It would be a new school record!

In the final group, some of the little ones had already given up. Some had hardly eaten anything at all. One little girl was crying because nobody told her it was blueberry, and she hated blueberry. But one little first grader looked like he had never been fed. The crowd did not know, however, that he had just eaten a Filet-o-Fish and a large fries for lunch, and when he finished his pie, he'd probably ask the child next to him if he could finish hers too.

The crowd began chanting, "Stevie! Stevie! Stevie! Stevie!"

Stevie took a break, sat up, smiled, and looked around at all the people. Then he took a deep breath, bent over, ate his last bite of apple filling, jumped up on the bench, and posed like Arnold Schwarzenegger.

Everyone laughed.

My mom put her head in her hands. Mr. Mason stood behind Stevie and grabbed his arm.

"And Stevie wins!" he shouted into the megaphone. "That's a sweep for the Done boys!"

The crowd went wild. They hoisted all three of us boys onto the table and gave each of us a first-place ribbon. The president of the PTA took photos. A few moments later she presented my mom with a special ribbon.

It said, "Mother of the Three Little Pigs."

# Writing

*"Boys and girls,"* I announced, "today we are going to learn how to write."

Justin groaned.

Then I said, "Now put your coats and hats on. We are going outside."

"Yeah!" they all screamed.

"But there is one rule," I said. "You may not say one word when we go outside. Got it?"

They smiled and nodded with their mouths closed.

We put on our coats and hats and lined up. Then we walked outside in single file to an open field right next to our school. No one spoke.

We sat down in the grass, closed our eyes, and listened to children shout in the distant playground. We lay down on our backs and took big breaths and tried to smell the wetness of autumn. We watched golden leaves say good-bye to branches and followed their paths to the ground. We waited for the leaves to fall on our faces.

It began to drizzle. They all looked at me, expecting me to say it's time to go back inside. We didn't. The children looked at each other with wide eyes. We took our hats off instead, and tried to catch raindrops in our mouths. They were dying to speak, but no one did. For they knew it would break the spell.

"OK, everyone," I said, "let's walk back to class."

We kicked rocks and crunched leaves on our way back to school. We slipped in mud and splashed in puddles. We felt the cold autumn earth through our shoes. Finally we walked inside, took off our coats, wiped our feet, and hung up our hats. Everyone sat down. They all looked at me. Peter raised his hand. His lips were held tight.

"Yes, Peter?" I said. "You may speak now."

He let out a big sigh and put his hand down.

"Mr. Done," he asked, "when are we going to learn how to write?"

I smiled. "You just did, Peter. You just did."

# Garage Sales

*OK, I admit it.* I'm cheap. Before leaving a hotel, I grab all the soap—and the shoehorns and the shower caps. I don't need to buy any cologne because I have hundreds of those little samples you get on index cards at the cologne counter. My friends won't go out to dinner with me anymore because they're embarrassed by my coupon book. When I go grocery shopping, I eat all the little pizza samples that the lady at the end of the frozen food aisle is giving away. And the best present anyone ever gave me was from my brother Steve—a gift certificate to the Salvation Army Store.

So what if I take the barf bags from the plane (they make terrific lunch bags)? I have to be frugal. All teachers have to be. How else can we afford to buy everything we need for school?

Actually, over the years I have become very good at bargain hunting and have fallen in love with garage sales. Every Friday night I scour the local paper for the next day's sales. I circle the ones that look promising and check the addresses on the map. On Saturday mornings I wake up at five, fill up my big travel mug with coffee, and hit the road.

If I see a garage sale sign, I look for bicycles on the lawn, or a basketball hoop over the garage, or a lemonade stand on the curb.

Bicycles and basketball hoops and lemonade stands mean kids. And kids mean kids' stuff. And kids' stuff means books and checker sets and puzzles for rainy day recess.

One day I was driving along a street when I saw a lady just opening up her garage for the sale. I spotted roller skates on the porch, a soccer ball in the tree, and a hula hoop in the hall closet. (My sense for spotting kids' toys is highly developed.) I parked my car and walked up to her garage.

The nice lady was selling off a ton of her kids' stuff. I figured they had either just gone off to college or she was very mad at them.

I walked over to one of the boxes, put down my coffee mug, and started to shake. The boxes were filled with *Madeline*s and *Babar*s, and *Encyclopedia Brown*s and *Nancy Drew*s in almost perfect condition! This was better than Vegas! But I did not jump up and down. It is always best to remain calm when you find a box of children's books with no price tags.

Suddenly I spotted a heavy-set lady grabbing books out of another box. She had a giant coffee mug too. She was putting books into a totebag. Her sack had thirty names on it. The names were written with glitter glue.

I knew it! Another teacher.

I turned over a box of stuffed animals and began filling it with books. The teacher with the totebag spotted me and started grabbing faster. I did not like that she was getting anything. So I stood up and walked over to her. She gave me a dirty look and tried to cover up the books in her bag.

Then I reached down and pulled a copy of *Amelia Bedelia* out of the box. It was only ten cents! She grabbed it out of my hands.

"Hey!" I screamed. "Gimme that!"

"I had it first," screamed the Mean Teacher.

"You did not!" I yelled.

"Yes, I did," yelled Mean Teacher again.

"It's mine!" I shouted.

"It is not!" screamed Mean Teacher. "I was here first. Go back to your own box."

She would not let go.

Just then the Nice Lady came over and said, "If you two are interested in children's things, I have more over here." And she pointed to three big boxes under a picnic table. We both ran over to the table.

Eureka! There was a globe and a chemistry set and a rock tumbler and Legos and Junior Scrabble. There were children's dictionaries, and boxes of multiplication flash cards, and jump ropes, and a set of children's encyclopedias, and Twister, and Battleship, and Chutes and Ladders, and a big plastic clock for learning how to tell time.

"I'll take it all," said the Mean Teacher calmly.

"Hey!" I yelled. "I want it!"

"Oh my." The Nice Lady laughed nervously. "I guess I should sell it to the lady who said she wanted it first."

"What?" I screamed. "That's not fair."

Mean Teacher smiled. "How much?" she asked.

"Well . . . is five dollars too much?" asked Nice Lady.

"Five dollars?" I yelled. I started gagging.

You will *not* believe what happened next.

Mean Teacher said, "Will you take four?"

I grabbed my chest.

"Well . . . OK," said Nice Lady.

I fell on the driveway.

Four dollars for all that! This was robbery! Not only was Mean Teacher mean—she was a *thief!* Imagine asking for a discount, when she was already getting everything for nothing!

Then Mean Teacher asked Nice Lady to help her carry everything to her car. This was too much. I crawled away. While they were loading up Mean Teacher's car, I spotted *Amelia Bedelia* on the picnic bench. Mean Teacher must have forgotten it. Ha! I thought. And I grabbed it.

After Mean Teacher drove away, I walked up to Nice Lady and held out the book. I smiled.

"Will you take five cents?"

# Sharing

*Do you think* Joshua's mother knows that we all heard how grouchy she is now that she is on Weight Watchers? Does Sean's dad know that we all heard exactly what he said to his mother-in-law about her Jell-O salad? Maybe Ryan's dad doesn't want us to know that he slept on the couch last night. And perhaps Emily's mom would rather we didn't all hear that she cries every time she watches *Baywatch*.

Whenever I hear something I probably shouldn't, I cringe and wonder just what they go home and say about me. But I'm prepared. If the parents ask, I just say, "You believe half of what your child says about me, and I'll believe half of what I hear about you."

My sister-in-law was *thrilled* when her daughter told her whole class that Mommy cried all night because her Miss Clairol was too red. And my brother, Carl, was *very happy* when his youngest son announced to his classmates that Daddy drives ninety miles per hour on the freeway. He was also *so glad* to hear that the whole class learned that Daddy just got his second speeding ticket this month and tried to sweet-talk his way out of it.

Parents be warned. Kids share everything.

My students live for three things: recess, lunch, and sharing.

It is true. What's worse is they think the days of the week are Monday, Tuesday, Wednesday, Thursday, and Shareday.

I have spent most of the Sharedays of my life clapping for Lego inventions, holding hamsters, admiring swimming medals, playing Try to Find Me in team soccer photos, and getting excited about old stuffed animals, Pinewood Derby cars, and turtles that don't move.

But it's not all stuffed animals and hamsters and turtles. Sometimes it's pretty darn entertaining.

Once I had a student named Andrea who walked up to the front of the class and announced, "My mom went off the pill, and now I am going to have a baby brother."

Once Greg told the class that the police came to his house last night and took away all his parents' potted plants.

And one year Heidi held up her mom's ultrasound photo of her soon-to-arrive baby brother and explained in great detail why it's a boy.

Every year I select winners for the best sharing of the year. Oh, I don't tell the kids. But I do tell my friends. This year Jenny took third place.

"What are you going to share today, Jenny?" I asked one Shareday.

"Well," she said, "my mother was having a dinner party on Saturday night and she had a lot of people over, and my little brother was walking around during the party, and my mom noticed that he was bumping into the furniture and falling on the floor, so she asked one of the guests, who is a doctor, to look at my brother and see what is wrong with him, and the doctor said that my brother was drunk!"

"Now, Jenny," I said skeptically, "come on. Your brother is two years old."

"It's true!" she said. "You can ask my mom."

And she continued, "You see, before dinner everyone was standing around having cocktails and they were all giving my little brother the cherries from their drinks, and my mom figured out that he had eaten about ten cherries in one hour, and they were full of alcohol, so my little brother got drunk."

Joey yelled out, "My uncle got drunk at my aunt's wedding and—"

"Thank you, Joey," I said. I turned back to Jennifer. "Thank you too, Jenny. You may sit down now."

This year's second place winner was Emily. She brought in her dog.

"What's your dog's name?" I asked.

"Meatloaf," she answered.

Emily told us how old Meatloaf was, where they got him, and what he eats. She showed us all how Meatloaf sits and how he lies down. Then she turned him around.

"These aren't his real testicles," she announced.

I froze.

"They're plastic," Emily said.

All the kids leaned in to see Meatloaf's implants.

"He doesn't know he's missing anything though," she continued. "He thinks they're real."

I looked down.

"They're called Neuticles," she explained.

I shook my head.

"When Meatloaf was fixed, my dad wanted them put in. My dad says Meatloaf is a boy and he should look like one."

"They look real," said Joshua.

I thanked both Emily and Meatloaf. Unfortunately their time was up.

This year's blue ribbon went to Ryan.

One Shareday Ryan walked up to the front of the classroom carrying a burlap bag.

"What did you bring to share today, Ryan?" I asked.

He held up the bag. "Guess!" he said, smiling.

We all guessed.

"OK, Ryan," I said, "we've all tried to guess. Now tell us what it is."

He smiled. "Ladybugs," he said proudly.

"Ryan, come on," I said.

"No really," he said. "It's ladybugs. My uncle is a farmer. He orders ladybugs every year and puts them out in the crops."

"Ryan," I said slowly. "You cannot just order ladybugs."

"Yeah, you can," he said. "Look!"

And he untied the rope.

Immediately swarms of ladybugs flew out of the bag. Everyone started screaming and jumped out of their seats trying to catch them.

"Ryan, close that bag!" I screamed.

"I told you so," he said.

*"Close that bag!"*

# Out for a Day

*I hate writing sub plans.* By the time I've written everything down for the substitute, I might as well have stayed at school and taught myself. It takes me hours just to write down where everything is, who is on medication, who is allergic to what, who should not sit next to whom, where everyone needs to go for ESL and learning resource and speech and detention, and "If Stephen says he has to go to the bathroom, let him!"

I always get nervous when I've been out for a day and read the note from the sub. Last time I was out, Anthony and Carlos switched their name tags, Justin went out to wipe mud off of his shoes and never returned, Peter pretended that he only spoke Polish, Anthony (playing Carlos) said he broke his glasses and couldn't see the math problems on the board (Anthony doesn't wear glasses), and Emily said she was allergic to binder paper.

Once a friend of mine who teaches middle school went on maternity leave. The students in her homeroom class were so bad that the substitute just up and left one day without telling anyone. Now, this particular group of students was a clever bunch. They knew that if they tore the room apart, someone would find out immediately. So each day they copied math problems out of their math books, wrote in their journals, and read their silent reading books. When the principal stopped by, the kids said that the teacher had just run to the bathroom. They pulled it off for three days, until the principal finally checked.

I have become very good at deciphering substitutes' notes.

"They are quite an enthusiastic group." They were wild.

"They are very social." They would not shut up.

"They are an opinionated bunch." They whined all day.

"They sure seemed hungry." They fooled her into opening the snack drawer.

"Is Stephen on medication?" Sub will not be returning.

It's not easy being out of the classroom. When I have a sub, I sit at home and stare at the clock all day long. "It's eight thirty," I say to myself, "They're walking in right now." "It's eight forty-five. They're handing in their homework." "It's ten now. Justin is staying in at recess doing his homework."

Nowadays, if I know I'm going to be away, I bribe them.

"Boys and girls," I say, "if you are all really, really good while I'm away tomorrow, I will take you out for extra PE."

I also leave detailed plans for the sub.

"Welcome to our class! Recess begins at 10:00 a.m., not 9:00. Recess is 20 minutes long, not 60. They may *not* eat sunflower seeds during math time. We do *not* practice our spelling words on the jungle gym. They may *not* play with their Game Boys during silent reading even if they promise to be quiet. There *is* homework tonight! We are *not* in the middle of a *Star Wars* film festival. And Brian may *not* order take-out pizza on his cell phone."

Sometimes it is not the students who worry me. It is the substitute. I get scared when I come back after being out for a day, and the kids say they had the *best* day of their lives.

The last time I came back after being gone, I asked everyone, "How'd it go yesterday?"

"Super!" Peter answered.

"How did you like having Mrs. Black as a sub?" I asked.

"She's great!" said Melanie.

"Yeah, she was so nice," said Emily.

"Why was she so nice?" I asked nervously.

"She let us play dodgeball," said Justin.

"Dodgeball!" I screamed. "I didn't write that you could play dodgeball. When did you play dodgeball?"

"After recess," answered Carlos.

"That's math time!" I yelled. "Didn't you do fractions yesterday?"

"No," answered Patrick.

"How long did you play dodgeball?" I asked.

"Till lunch," said Amanda.

"That's two hours!" I shouted. "Didn't Mrs. Black review nouns, verbs, and adjectives with you yesterday?"

"What's a noun?" asked Natalie.

"What did you do after lunch?" I asked.

"She played her ukulele," said Jenny.

"She *what?*" I screamed.

"And she showed us her slides of Mount Kilauea," Melissa said.

"Can we have our extra PE now?" asked Peter.

"Are you kidding? You had your extra PE with Mrs. Black!" I shouted.

"But you promised!" said Aaron.

"No way," I said, "Besides, how do you know you got a good report?"

"She said she would give us one," said Carlos.

"Yeah, I'd get a good report too if I went on a *hukilau* all day long!" I shouted.

Peter raised his hand.

"Yes, Peter?" I asked.

"Mr. Done, are you OK?"

"Why, what's wrong?"

"You don't look so good," said Peter. "Maybe you should take another day off."

"Yeah," Melanie joined in. "You look sick. You should take tomorrow off and rest."

"You know," I nodded, "that's not a bad idea. Maybe you're right. I am not feeling my best."

I coughed really loud.

"In fact," I continued, "I think I *will* take tomorrow off." I coughed again. "And I think I will get Mr. Thompson to sub."

"*No!*" they all screamed.

"We want Mrs. Black," said Peter.

"Oh, didn't I tell you? I'm sorry. I must have forgotten. Mrs. Black is busy for the rest of the year. She's giving ukulele concerts in her muumuu at Mount Kilauea. You're absolutely right. A day off would be good for me. I'll get Mr. Thompson."

"No, please not Mr. Thompson!" screamed Peter.

"Not Mr. Thompson!" Justin pleaded. "He makes us do math."

Melanie spoke up. "You know what, Mr. Done? You're looking a lot better all of a sudden."

"Yeah," said Emily.

"You look great, Mr. Done!" said Peter. "Right everybody?"

Everyone shouted, "Right!"

Peter continued, "Mr. Done, you're our favorite teacher. In fact, you're the best teacher in the whole wide world."

He paused.

"Now can we have PE?" he asked.

I smiled and looked around the room. I waited, and then, "OK," I said.

Everyone shouted.

So, I'm a sucker. I admit it.

But hey, they did get a good report.

# Parent-Teacher Conferences

*Yesterday was* Parent-Teacher Conference Day. Cathy put survival kits in all of our mailboxes. They contained lozenges for sore throats, Excedrin for headaches, chocolate for energy—and for courage, purple hearts cut out of construction paper.

The dads won again. You see, every year I take a little survey to see who the kids resemble more—their moms or their dads. Dads have won for three straight years. Jenny has her dad's ears. Anthony has his dad's belly. And now I know exactly what Peter will look like without any hair. Nicole's mom says it just isn't fair. The moms do all the work, and the kids end up looking like their fathers.

The little apples in my class do not fall far from their trees. Kevin's mom said that math is not her strong subject either. Sarah's dad struggled in reading too. And Matthew's mom said he inherited his bad spelling from her.

I tried to explain that Joshua has some attention difficulties, but I don't think his dad heard me. He kept looking around the room. And I told Ji Soo's mom that Ji Soo seems stressed out. She can't sleep at night worrying about him.

I wanted to tell Peter's mom that Peter is talking too much in class, but I couldn't get a word in. And I was all prepared to speak with Carlos's parents about his attendance problems, but they never showed up.

When I was a child, I always got nervous before conference day. I remember the little note that came home saying, "Your child has a conference on such and such a date." It was always on a half sheet of goldenrod paper, and we had to get it signed and returned the very next day or the teacher would get upset, and you didn't want that to happen because then she might not say nice things about you at the conference.

I remember that I always wrote extra neatly during conference week just in case my teacher showed my papers to my mom. And I remember trying to listen through the little window next to the classroom door to hear what my teachers were saying.

When my mom walked out of her conference, I always begged her to tell me what the teachers said. But my mom would never say much. She wasn't one to talk about such things. She didn't put report cards on the refrigerator either.

Most of my own students are just like I was. Sometimes they look panicked as their parents walk into the conference and they wait out in the hall.

"Amanda, relax!" I say.

"Brian, smile! It's not the end of the world."

"Katie, don't look so frightened. Why don't you go clean out your cubby."

Like I was, they are dying to know what happens after their parents walk into the classroom.

And so—I will tell.

I see your mom sit down nervously, then hear her sigh when I explain that you are so well behaved in class.

I catch the corners of your dad's mouth go up when I tell him how much your English has improved, and see his chest swell when I show him the 100 percent on your addition test.

I watch your mom smile when I describe how you sat by the new student at lunch without being asked, and notice her put her hand on your father's knee when I tell them how hard you work in class.

I move my chair as your parents lean in to read your story, and hear them both laugh when they get to the part about your teacher's being attacked by coffee cups.

I see them shake their heads when they look inside your desk, and am glad they didn't look in mine.

I watch them beam as they get up to leave—proud of your good work, and proud to be your parents.

# Report Cards

*Most teachers' least favorite time* of year is report card time. Personally, I would rather zip up all the kindergarteners' snowsuits for a month than write reports.

Oh, some are easy. It's the delicate ones that are difficult to write. And sometimes I just don't know what to say.

Take Brian's report, for example. How am I going to tell his parents that Brian will not sit still?

"Dear Mr. Walters, please send glue gun."

And what do I write about Peter?

"May I please use masking tape on your son's mouth?"

Probably not a good idea.

Several years ago, after I handed in my report cards for review, Cathy brought them all back.

"What's wrong?" I asked.

"You have to change these," she said.

"Why?"

"They're too direct."

"What do you mean?" I asked.

"Well," Cathy continued, "look at this one, for example." She pulled out Cindy's report.

"Yeah," I asked. "What's wrong with it?"

"You can't write, 'Cindy has a big mouth,' " she said.

"But she does."

"I know she does, but you can't write that," Cathy explained.

"Why not?"

"You have to be gentler," she said. "And look here." She showed me Lauren's report.

"What's wrong with hers?" I asked.

"You can't say, 'Lauren is a big baby.' "

"But she is."

Cathy handed me the stack. "Change them."

"OK," I said grudgingly.

Soon Cindy "needed to develop quieter habits of communication," and Lauren "exhibited a lack of maturity in her relationships."

Since then I haven't had any problems with my reports. Well, till this year, that is. Yesterday Cathy came by my room before school. She held up one of my report cards.

"Uh-oh," I said. "I know what this means."

She smiled. "It's only one," she said meekly.

"Good," I said. "Which one?"

"Justin's."

"Justin's? Why?"

"Well," she said, "you wrote that Justin eats with his mouth open all the time. Can you say something a bit . . . *nicer?*"

"That *is* nice," I said. "Have you ever seen him eat?"

"There's got to be a nicer way to say this," she said.

"What do you want me to say?"

"I don't know. Maybe something like 'Justin needs to develop his social graces,' " she suggested.

I shook my head. "That's too vague."

"How about 'Justin needs to exhibit better table manners at lunch'?" she said.

"How about 'Justin should hold a mirror when he eats and see what he looks like'?" I laughed.

"Phil!" she groaned.

"OK, OK. Give it to me. I'll fix it," I said. And she left.

Later in the day, I walked into Cathy's office and handed her Justin's report. "It's the best I could do," I said.

She read it: "Justin should never sit across from anyone at mealtimes."

I smiled. "What do you think?"

She threw her hands up and said, "You're hopeless. I give up! Just leave it the way you originally had it. But if Justin's parents call me, I'm sending them to *you!*"

# Why?

*Why can kids say,* "Jinks, one, two, three, four, five, six, seven, eight, nine, ten—you owe me a Coke," in less than .05 seconds but take three hours to tell me what eight times seven is?

Why will kids ask me ten times when recess is but then stay in for the whole break organizing all the markers and cleaning the whiteboard with too much whiteboard spray?

Why is the gumball machine in the museum lobby more interesting than the Van Gogh on loan from the Met?

Why don't we grade A, B, C, D, and E?

Why do kids forget where to indent in a letter but remember the name of my guinea pig I had when I was in third grade, and why my dad washed my mouth out with soap when I was eight?

Why do kids write "THE END" so big?

Why do kids know precisely how many days, hours, and minutes are left till their birthdays but still ask, "When's lunch?"

Why do kids complain when they have to run in PE, but can run around the neighborhood for three straight hours while wearing a refrigerator box on Halloween night?

Why do the pistols in my class always gravitate toward each other like magnets?

Why do they notice the shaving cream in my ears this morning but not see the muddy footprints going all the way to their desks?

Why do kids choose to play band instruments that are similar to their own personalities?

Why is it that they can't figure out how to put their homework into their three-ring binders, but when I can't get the VCR to work, they can fix it?

Why can't kids remember to bring back their field trip notes, but can remember to bring the whoopie cushion and the plastic dog poop and the plastic rat on April Fool's Day?

Why are there so many holes in the pencil sharpener?

Why is it that kids can't see that there are no periods or capitals in their four-page story but notice that my socks do not match this morning?

Why do all the animals decide it's time to make babies when we visit the zoo?

Why, when there are 20,000 books in the library, do they just want *I Spy?*

Why can't kids tell me twelve minus nine, when they can figure out exactly how old I am in less than two seconds when I tell them the year I was born?

Why do my students just stare at me and say nothing when they run into me in the supermarket?

Why do kids not hear the directions I have already repeated five times, but hear every word I just whispered to the librarian about why I have a headache this morning?

# Halloween

*Do you know* which question teachers are most commonly asked? I will give you a clue. Students begin asking this question around the first week of school and keep asking it all the way up to the end of October. Can you guess what it is? I will tell you. The most commonly asked question of teachers is "What are you going to be for Halloween?"

This year I have already been asked the question seventy-five times. I counted. Fifty of those times I was asked by Joey.

My answer is always the same. "It's a surprise." I smile. But of course when I say this, I am lying. I really do not have the foggiest idea what I am going to be. In fact, I never know what I am going to be till the night before Halloween, when I empty my closet out onto my bed and try to put a costume together out of dress shirts and a bathrobe and ties.

This year, Michael was the first to run in on Halloween Day.

"Mr. Done, when can we put our costumes on?" Michael shouted.

"After lunch."

"When's that?"

"In three hours."

"Please can we put our costumes on?"

"No, Michael. You have to wait."

"Till when?"

"After lunch."

"Then can we put our costumes on?"

"Yes."

"When's lunch?"

"In three hours."

"But some kids have their costumes on already."

"Maybe so, but we're waiting."

"Till when?"

"After lunch."

"Then can we put our costumes on?"

"Yes."

"When's lunch?"

This Halloween I had bathroom duty. It was my job to stand in a small square space with all the third grade boys in the whole school and make sure nobody turned off the lights while they sprayed their hair green, covered their cheeks with Dracula blood, and put on their ninja and Grim Reaper masks.

As we waited on the blacktop for the parade to begin, I broke up sword fights, confiscated spears, and played Guess Who Is Under the Mask with all the ninjas and Grim Reapers.

Finally, the "Monster Mash" tape started playing through the loudspeakers and the parade began. I marched with Justin and waved to all the mommies while they pointed at me and laughed, and tried to figure out how to use their new digital cameras.

"Mr. Done, what are you supposed to be?" Erika's mom, holding her video camera, screamed from the sidelines.

"A tired teacher," I answered.

"Weren't you that last year?"

"I was tired then too."

After the parade, it was time for the big party. Stephen and Brian ate their cupcakes with Dracula teeth in their mouths. Isabel and Melanie used seventeen rolls of toilet paper to win Wrap Up the Teacher Like a Mummy. And I bobbed for apples right after Joey sneezed in the water.

Then Mrs. Stewart and Mrs. Turner, my room moms, had everyone get into teams of four to play Frankenstein Makeup, and I watched my whole class paint each other's faces with peanut butter and mayonnaise and ketchup and toothpaste and shaving cream and jelly to create that authentic Frankenstein look. I watched the carpet get that authentic Frankenstein look too.

Frankly, I'd take three Christmas parties and four Easters any day for one Halloween. Whoever thought that stuffing millions of children with candy, then sticking them in costumes and putting spears in their hands all on the same day was a good idea?

Is it OK to call in sick on Halloween? Is it wrong to leave Frankenstein Makeup for your sub? Teachers catch colds in October, too, right?

# Teacher Speeches

*All teachers have* their standard speeches that they give during the year. Last year I started cataloging mine.

Sometimes I feel like a broken record. It would be so much easier if I could just shout out the number of the speech. For example, if I shouted, "Forty-seven!" they would know that they may get a drink. If I yelled, "Fifty-six!" they would know that they may go to the library. If I screamed, "Three seventy-three!" they would know that they may not take the bunny outside in the rain. It would save so much time.

Following are the speeches I give most often during the year.

## Speech 237—The Field Trip Speech

*"Today we are going on a field trip. You are all representatives of your school. Please behave. Please do not put your hands out of the windows of the bus and try to fly. Please do not try to make every truck that passes by honk. Please do not sing the complete 'One Hundred Bottles of Beer on the Wall.' Please remember that someone is driving your vehicle. Please remember that your driver needs the volume in the car to be under five hundred decibels in order to concentrate."*

## Speech 28—The Don't Touch Speech

*"Do not touch anything in the museum. Who did not hear me? Let's all say it together, 'We will not touch anything in the museum.' Good."*

## Speech 29—The Come Stand by Me Speech

*"I told you not to touch anything in the museum! Come stand by me."*

## Speech 45—The Stop Talking Speech

*"Excuse me, but I do not see a teapot on your desk. I don't see any cucumber sandwiches or scones. This is not a tea party. Now please stop talking, and get back to work."*

## Speech 38—The Don't Do It Just Because She Said to Speech

*"If she told you to jump off the Golden Gate Bridge, would you do that too?"*

## Speech 16—The Report Card Speech

*"Grades do not matter. I do not care if you get straight Fs. What matters is that you are trying your best."*

## Speech 17—The Do Your Best Speech

*"Is this your best work? No, it is not. Do you want a bad grade on your report card?"*

## Speech 178—The Homework Speech

*"There are only three things you have to do in life: 1) pay your taxes, 2) die, and 3) do your homework. Understand?"*

## Speech 479—The Make Mistakes Speech

*"Do not say 'Sorry' when you make a mistake. Never say 'Sorry' if you make a mistake. I want you to make mistakes. If you make mistakes, then I have something to teach you. And if I have something to teach you, then I keep my job. And if I have a job, then I can buy new ties at J. C. Penney."*

## Speech 65—The Get It Finished Speech

*"You have a zero in the gradebook. Do you know what that means? If you do not finish your book report, the zero turns into a bad grade, and if you get a lot of bad grades, you do not go to fourth grade, and if you do not go to fourth grade, you do not go on to fifth grade, and if you do not finish fifth grade, they will not let you into college, and if you do not go to college, you will not get a job. And if you do*

*not get a job, you cannot buy dog food. So if you want a dog someday, do your book report!"*

## Speech 258—The Sit on the Bench Speech

*"How would you like it if I called you names? I don't want to ever hear you saying bad words again. Now say you're sorry. Then go sit down on the bench, and don't get up till I say you can."*

## Speech 259—Oops

*"Sorry. I forgot you were on the bench. You can go back to class now."*

# Storytime

*Storytime* is my favorite part of the day. Every day after lunch, I love to gather my students around me on the carpet and read to them.

One day I started reading one of my all-time favorite books, *Dr. Jekyll and Mr. Hyde.* I have read it a dozen times before and know almost every line by heart. If I do say so myself, the part of Edward Hyde is one of my better roles.

When the children were all seated around me, I opened the book slowly and began reading in a low whisper. I was Vincent Price. The children sat silent. Sarah's eyes were glued on me. Kenny stopped fidgeting with his shoelace. James stopped playing with the Velcro on his sneaker. Natalie stopped braiding Nicole's hair.

As the story progressed, I continued to speak in low, haunting tones, gradually intensifying my speech for the best dramatic effect. Uta Hagen would have been proud.

Emily grabbed Amanda's arm. Justin did not know he was holding my shoe. It was going great. They were riveted by my performance.

I was approaching my favorite scene, the part where Edward Hyde takes his first sip of the magic drug that transforms him into Henry Jekyll. The children stared at my hand as I pretended to put three spoonfuls of the magic powder into a glass.

"There," I whispered in a scratchy voice. "It is complete."

Justin shivered.

I looked down at the children and laughed an evil laugh. I was Boris Karloff.

"Now," I continued in a heavy voice, "I must drink the magic drug."

I stood up slowly from my chair and gave an evil grin. The children leaned back. They stared at the imaginary glass in my hands as I lifted the smoking, blood-red liquid above my head. I looked down at the children one last time. I was John Barrymore. Slowly, I put the glass to my lips.

Suddenly a loud sound exploded from the center of the carpet. The room erupted with laughter. Peter pointed at Sarah. Justin held his nose.

"I didn't know girls could fart!" Justin shouted.

I fell back into my chair. I could not go on. My greatest theatrical moment ruined by a toot.

From then on, I decided, storytime would be *before* lunch.

# Ronny

*The other day after lunch,* I was listening to Ronny read. As usual, he didn't want to. Today we began a new book together. About halfway through, Ronny looked up at me and asked, "Mr. Done, what's your favorite word?"

I stared at him.

"You know something, Ronny," I said, "nobody's ever asked me that before. I never thought about it."

Ronny went back to his book. While he read, I thought about his question.

I have a favorite restaurant and ice cream and movie and book. So why don't I have a favorite word?

Words are my life. All day long I preach that *explained* and *screamed* and *whispered* are better than boring old *said*, and *wine* and *burgundy* and *garnet* are better than plain old *red*. The more I thought about it, the more I knew I needed to pick a favorite word. In fact, every teacher should have one.

But how does one go about picking a favorite from so many? Is it as simple as picking something I love—like *pizza*, or *history*, or *traveling*, or *Gershwin?* Maybe it just needs to sound nice— like *retirement*.

I asked Ronny for help. "Ronny, what is your favorite word?"

"*Whatchamacallit,*" he replied.

I smiled. "That is a mighty fine word," I said. "I like it."

"You can't have it," said Ronny. "It's my word. You have to have your own favorite word."

This was not going to be easy, I thought.

Well, I certainly knew what words it would not be. It would not be *treadmill* or *diet*. It might be *cruise,* or *summer,* or *sabbatical.*

I asked Ronny if I may have two favorite words.

He said yes.

*Bus duty* was definitely out. So was *yard duty.* It could be *mashed potatoes* or *sleeping in. Cleaning lady* and *beef Stroganoff* and *Justin's absent* sounded good too. Oh, it was so hard to choose.

After a couple of minutes, Ronny finished reading, closed his book, and looked up at me.

"Mr. Done?" he said.

"Yes, Ronny?"

He smiled. "I like reading now," he said.

I leaned in. "Ronny, may I have four favorite words?"

"Uh-huh," he said.

"I just heard you say them."

# The Happy Birthday Play

*Every month* I have the exact same conversation with my students. In fact, I have had the following conversation so many times that I have the script completely memorized.

*Setting:* My classroom
*Characters (in order of appearance):*
Student
Teacher
Classmates

### SCENE ONE

**STUDENT:** (Enters classroom carrying big white box. Lays box on my desk.) Hi, Mr. Done. My mom sent in treats for my birthday. When can we eat them?

**TEACHER:** (sarcastic) On the last day of school!

**STUDENT:** Come on! When?

**TEACHER:** OK, OK. At the end of the day.

**STUDENT:** (begging) Can we have them now? Please?

**TEACHER:** No.

**STUDENT:** (continues begging) Please!

**TEACHER:** (firmly) No!

| | |
|---|---|
| **STUDENT:** | (whining) Why not? |
| **TEACHER:** | (looks at student) Do you know what happens to little boys and girls when they eat cupcakes? |
| **STUDENT:** | What? |
| **TEACHER:** | (smiles sarcastically) They do not sit in their chairs. That's what. They do not stop talking. They think they are kites and begin to fly around the room. |
| **STUDENT:** | We'll be good. Promise! |
| **TEACHER:** | (with drama) Ha! Kites do not listen to the teacher. Kites do not like to do math. Do you know why your mom dropped you off today and left immediately? |
| **STUDENT:** | Why? |
| **TEACHER:** | (leans in to student) Because she also knows what will happen to you after you eat your cupcake. (Rest of class crosses their hands on their desks and sits motionless. Teacher looks at students.) Don't think for a second that you can all sit there like sweet little angels and think I'll change my mind. (Looks at box. Looks back at student.) What kind of cupcakes are they? |
| **STUDENT:** | Chocolate with chocolate frosting and chocolate sprinkles. You can have two. |
| **TEACHER:** | (Teacher looks around room. No one moves. Teacher looks at box. Teacher looks around room again.) Oh . . . all right. |
| **CLASSMATES:** | (loudly) Yeah! |
| **STUDENT:** | Thanks, Mr. Done. Why did you change your mind? |
| **TEACHER:** | I'd rather eat cupcakes than do math too. |

# When to Stop Teaching

*This November* I got a student teacher. Her name is Amy. She is twenty-two. The other day Amy gave her very first lesson in front of the class. Everything was going along nicely until a spider crawled across Katie's desk. Suddenly Katie jumped onto her chair and started screaming. Everyone ran over to Katie's desk to see the spider. When they saw the spider (which was three millimeters long), they all ran away, yelling and jumping onto their chairs and desks.

Amy stopped teaching and looked over at me with a what-do-I-do-now look. She must have missed this lesson in Teacher School, I thought. Or perhaps they don't teach this in Teacher School anymore. So I decided to make a list of instructions for Amy and anyone else who needs them.

The following things are guaranteed to bring any lesson to a grinding halt. If you happen to encounter any of these surprises while you are teaching, follow the directions below. If you are a student teacher, you have permission to photocopy these pages.

## Spiders

When a student screams, "Spider!" go directly to cup. Do not try to teach. Go directly to cup. Watch children jump out of seats and run to spider. Watch children jump backward when they see spider. Hear them scream loudly. Turn cup upside down. Capture spider. Put spider outside. Tell children to sit down. Tell children to sit down again. Then tell children to sit down and stay down. Listen to spider stories for twenty minutes.

## Fire Alarms

When you hear the fire alarm, line kids up. Tell kids to stop talking. Walk outside in single file. Tell kids to stop talking. Line up outside. Tell kids to stop talking. Answer "Is this a real fire?" five hundred times.

## Bees

When a bee flies in through the window, listen to children scream, "Bee!" over and over. Watch bee fly around room. Watch children fly around room also. Watch Justin start to swat bee. Scream, "Stop that!" Now, watch bee fly around room faster. Do not get cup. Bees do not like cups. Pick up folder. Try to shoo bee out of window with folder. Listen to children laugh at you as you try to shoo bee out the window. When bee is finally outside, listen to bee sting stories for twenty minutes.

## Wall Maps

If the wall map falls on you when you pull it down, stop teaching. Listen to children laugh. Try to hang the wall map back up. If you cannot hang the wall map back up, listen to children laugh louder. If you are successful in securing the wall map on the hooks, listen to children beg you to pull the map down again. Do not do it. This is a trick. They want the wall map to fall down on you again.

## Snow

When the first snow falls, listen to children scream, "Look! Snow!" Children will ask to go outside. Say no. Children will repeat question. Repeat answer. Warning: Do not walk near your coat or door at this time. If you do, children will think you are going outside and start jumping up and down and wagging their tails.

## Lightning

When you see lightning, children will begin to chatter. Do not say, "Quiet." It does not work. All children talk when they see lightning. You will soon hear thunder. Do not try to squeeze math problems in between lightning and thunder crashes. It does not work either.

## Power Outage

If the lights go out, stop teaching immediately. Find flashlight. If you cannot find flashlight, light candle. If candle sets off fire alarm, go outside. If you go outside and there is a snowstorm, go back inside. If lights are still out and bee does not fly into room, but spider crawls on student's desk and you cannot find the cup, take down wall map and go after spider.

# The Thanksgiving Feast

*Every November* Mrs. Wilson has a huge Thanksgiving feast in her room. For the first three weeks of November, I can hear her kids singing "Over the River and Through the Wood," while they cut vests out of brown paper bags, string macaroni necklaces, stick feathers into pinecone centerpieces, and pop popcorn (the first Thanksgiving had popcorn). Mrs. Wilson always brings the turkey.

Well, I always have a Thanksgiving feast in my room too. My Thanksgiving feast consists of one bag of Doritos and thirty-two plastic cups. We watch *Pocahontas*. The drinking fountain is in the hall.

But this year I decided to have a Thanksgiving feast just like Mrs. Wilson's. Everybody signed up to bring something. And *I* volunteered to cook the turkey.

Now, I had never cooked a turkey before in my life. Actually, I had never even bought a turkey before. When I was a kid, my mom always got up early on Thanksgiving and had the turkey in the oven before I woke up. I remember she would open the oven door every so often and squirt it with a squirter thing. I'm not sure why, but apparently you need it to cook a turkey.

So the day before our big feast, I drove to Safeway and

bought the biggest turkey I could find. It was twenty-five pounds. I bought a big aluminum pan and a squirter like Mom's, lugged it all home, and put the turkey in the fridge.

The next morning, I got up at five a.m. and took the bird out of the fridge. It was still frozen. I read the instructions on the label.

Cook at 300 degrees. A twenty-five-pound turkey needs six hours to cook.

Six hours! I had to leave for work in two.

I'll just cook it at a higher temperature, I thought. So I turned the oven up to 400, threw the turkey into the pan, popped the pan into the oven, got the squirter ready, and went to take a shower.

About 30 minutes later, I returned and opened the oven door.

Still frozen.

I filled the squirter with water, sprayed the whole bird, turned the dial up to 500, then left to get dressed.

In half an hour I returned, opened the oven door, and poked the turkey with a fork. Still frozen.

"Damn!" I said.

I had to leave for work in fifteen minutes and my turkey was still frozen. Maybe I'd bought a penguin.

Quickly I turned off the oven, threw the bird back into the fridge, and drove to Safeway. They had two small chickens on the rotisserie.

I looked at the chickens.

Hmm. I thought about it for a second. I could say they were baby turkeys.

No, Sarah would get hysterical. She cried when she found an egg that had fallen out of a tree. Baby turkeys would put her over the edge.

I rang for the butcher.

"Hi. I need a turkey for a Thanksgiving feast. Could you cook one and deliver it to my school?" I asked.

"When do you need it?" he asked.

"Today. At noon."

He laughed. "Sorry sir. Not enough time."

"Shoot!" I said.

I walked to the refrigerated aisle. A man was stocking shelves.

"Hi. Do you have any turkey meat?" I asked.

"Sorry. All out, sir," he answered.

"Darn. Any turkey dogs?"

"Nope. All out of those too. Ran out an hour ago."

"An hour ago?" I cried.

"Yes, sir. Are you a teacher?"

"Yeah. How'd you know?" I asked.

"You're the third one this morning."

A couple of hours later, we began setting up for the feast. The room moms removed aluminum foil and Saran Wrap from trays of carrot sticks and apple slices and cornbread and pumpkin pies and laid the food out on the tables. It was a big spread.

"Hey, Mr. Done, where's the turkey?" Michael asked.

"Yeah, where's the turkey?" asked Erika.

I paused. Everyone looked at me.

"Well, boys and girls . . . ," I said nervously.

I sighed, bent down, and pulled out a plastic bag from under my desk. I took a big breath.

"Everyone has turkey on Thanksgiving," I said. "That's boring. So today I decided we should be really authentic. Today, we are going to have"—I pulled them out of the bag—"hot dogs!"

*"Hot dogs?"* they all screamed.

"Sure!" I smiled. "What do you think Squanto ate with all that popcorn?"

# Out of Proportion

*Mike, Lisa, and I* flew to Rome over the Thanksgiving break. I flew free on my dad's frequent flyer miles. My friends loved the Sistine Chapel and the Colosseum and the Spanish Steps. Unfortunately, I did not see them. I was too busy in the souvenir shops.

I know. It's bad. Mike and Lisa say I have a problem. You see, whenever I go anywhere, I spend all my time in the souvenir shops. I can't stay away from them. But you should see my snow globes of the Sistine Chapel and the Colosseum and the Spanish Steps. They're beautiful.

Of course I don't buy all this for me. I buy it for school. You never know when you might need a placemat of the pope or two hundred slides of Saint Peter's, right?

When I returned home, I gathered my students on the carpet to tell them all about my trip.

"Guess where Mr. Done went for vacation?" I asked. "I'll give you a clue. It's in Italy."

"Rome?" Nicole guessed.

"Very good," I said.

I pulled down the world map (very carefully) and pointed to Italy.

"Now," I said, "one of the most famous artists who ever lived is a man named Michelangelo. Have any of you heard of Michelangelo?"

Emily raised her hand.

"Good, Emily. Now, many of Michelangelo's works are in Rome, and I saw some of them. And I brought some things to show you."

I pulled a poster out of my bag and unrolled it.

"This is the ceiling of the Sistine Chapel," I said.

"That's neat," said Kenny.

"Michelangelo painted this ceiling," I said and explained a little of the ceiling's history and what each panel on the ceiling represented.

"Now, boys and girls," I continued, "I learned some interesting things about Michelangelo's works when I was in Rome. When you look at some of his works, you will see that not everything is in proportion. Do you know what it means when something is 'out of proportion'?"

No answer.

"Well," I explained, "When something is out of proportion, that means that something is too big or too small in comparison to the other parts. For example, if you're looking at a statue of a person and the feet look too small, then we say the feet are 'out of proportion' with the rest of the body."

"Oh, I get it," Peter said.

"Now," I continued, "sometimes Michelangelo painted or sculpted out of proportion."

I pulled out a postcard of *David* (waist up).

"This is Michelangelo's *David,*" I explained. "Do you notice anything unusual?"

"His hand is too big," said Isabel.

"You're right, Isabel."

"Oh yeah," said Joshua.

"You see, David's hand is out of proportion," I said.

Next I pulled out a miniature statue of Michelangelo's *Pietà*.

"This is Michelangelo's *Pietà,*" I said. "Michelangelo sculpted it when he was very young. Now look at Mary's body. It is very big. If she were to stand up, she'd be very tall. Now look at her head."

"It's too small," said Nicole.

"You're absolutely right, Nicole. Mary's head is too small compared to the rest of her body. Her head is out of proportion. Everyone understand?"

"Uh-huh," they all answered.

Peter raised his hand.

"Yes, Peter?" I asked.

"Mr. Done, I see another place where Michelangelo is out of proportion," he said.

"You do?" I asked, surprised. "Where?"

"In the Sistine Chapel," said Peter.

"What do you mean?" I asked.

He hesitated.

"Uh . . . well . . . I don't mean to be naughty," Peter said slowly, "but isn't *that* out of proportion?" And he pointed right between Adam's legs.

I looked at the print. Peter was right. It *was* out of proportion.

Then Justin shouted, "It's too small!"

"Yeah, it's too small," said Matthew. "My dad's is—"

"Thank you, Matthew," I said, cutting him off. "That's your daddy's business."

"Mr. Done, your face is red," said Nicole.

"It's hot in here," I replied, loosening my tie. "Open the window."

"I'm not hot," Emily said.

I took a big breath.

"OK, everyone," I announced, "I think that's enough art history for the day. Back to your seats."

I knew I should have shown the snow globes.

# Airplane Trip

*On our flight home from Rome,* I had the funniest feeling that I was at school. Then it dawned on me. Being on an airplane is the same as being in the classroom.

First, the passengers walk in carrying their bags. They walk in single file. As they file in, flight attendants stand at the entrance and say, "Good morning." They are smiling.

The passengers put their bags into cubbies. They sit in rows. Some do not want to be sitting by the person who is seated next to them. Some of their knees do not fit under the tables.

The flight attendants walk down the aisles handing out papers and reading material. They look at your chair to see if you are seated properly. They answer questions and repeat themselves a lot. When they give the safety lesson, the passengers do not listen.

If you look around, you will see that some of the passengers are reading. Some are sleeping. Some are talking. Some are looking out the window. Hopefully no one is throwing up.

In the classroom the kids who need the most "attention" always sit by the teacher. In the plane the kids who need the most "attention" always sit by me too. It doesn't matter where I sit. They find me. I think that after I sit down, the flight attendant puts a sign over my seat that says, "He plays rock, paper, scissors."

During the flight, you have to sit while you eat your snack. You cannot use your cellphone. Your lunch comes on a tray. You cannot flush things down the toilet. And if you walk outside during the flight, you are in trouble.

When the flight is over, everyone wants to leave as soon as possible. But the passengers must remain seated until the flight attendants say they can go. When it is time to leave, some passengers push and shove. Some forget their coats.

The flight attendants stand at the front door again and say, "Good-bye," and, "Have a nice day!" They are smiling because they are happy that all the passengers are going home. Tomorrow they will do it all over again.

*Winter*

# The Looks

*One day* my student teacher Amy put her head down on her desk.

"What's the matter?" I asked.

"I don't think I'm cut out for this," she cried. She lifted her head up. "Justin is constantly out of his seat, Peter tried to turn me off with the remote, Sarah was crying again, Brian drew red dots all over himself and said he has the chicken pox, and right in the middle of my math lesson, you know what Carlos asked me?"

"What?" I asked.

"Do crocodiles have butts?"

I bit my lip. "Sounds normal." I smiled.

"I don't think I will ever be a teacher." She sighed.

"Sure you will," I said. "You're good. Listen, teaching is ninety percent natural and ten percent learned. You have the ninety percent. Now you just need to learn a few tools, that's all."

"But I don't know what to do," she cried. "I try, but sometimes they just won't listen."

"The problem is you don't have the looks down yet," I said.

"The what?"

"The looks," I repeated. "Every teacher has a collection of looks. You have to, or you won't survive."

"What do you mean?" she asked.

"Let me explain. Basically there are five different teacher looks. The first look is called the Raised Eyebrow."

"The what?"

"The Raised Eyebrow," I repeated. "It's easy. Simply raise both eyebrows as high as you can. Do not speak. Keep your head perfectly still. Stare at the child for five to ten seconds."

"When do you give the Raised Eyebrow?" Amy asked.

"When Justin is writing on his desk or Stephen is playing with his rubber band."

Amy grabbed a pen and began writing this down. I continued.

"The second look is the Chin Up. This one's a bit more difficult to master. For the Chin Up, raise your chin slowly. While you're raising your chin, raise your eyebrows at the same time."

I demonstrated.

"See?" I said.

"Yes," said Amy. She made some more notes. "But when do I use the Chin Up?"

"When Ronny stabs Brian with a paper clip on the way to the pencil sharpener, or Carlos tells Sarah to put her finger in the stapler."

"I see," Amy said.

"But don't confuse the Chin Up with the Chin Down," I said. "The Chin Down is for not doing your homework, or for emptying the pencil sharpener on the counter. When giving the Chin Down, tilt your head down till it touches your chest. Your lips will automatically pucker up a bit as you lower your chin. Raise your eyebrows and cock your chin slightly to the left. Stare at the student for three to five seconds. For greatest effect, stare over the rim of your glasses like this . . ."

I lowered my frames, lowered my chin, raised my eyebrows, and froze.

"See?" I said.

"Got it." Amy nodded. She kept writing.

I continued, "The fourth look is the Pursed Lip. To give the Pursed Lip, simply pucker your lips together tightly while staring at the student. Furl your eyebrows as hard as you can, and breathe in deeply so that the student hears you. But do not let the air out right away. Hold your breath for two to three seconds."

"When do I use the Pursed Lip?" Amy asked.

"When Brian pulls the fire alarm, or Joey uses the library windows as a ball wall," I answered.

"What's the last look?" Amy asked.

"The Jaw Drop," I answered. "This one's easy. Just open your mouth, look horrified, and freeze for three to five seconds. I gave the Jaw Drop twice last week—once when Joshua pushed Natalie into the boys' bathroom, and once when Melanie took Penelope outside without asking, then came back and told me she couldn't find her."

"Of course," I continued, "there are variations on all five looks. The Pursed Lip works well when tapping the desk or the whiteboard or the student's shoulder. The Raised Eyebrow is highly effective when accompanied with shouting the student's name. And the Jaw Drop is successful when you put both hands on your head. See?"

I demonstrated.

"Yes. Yes, I see," said Amy. "That's good."

"The Jaw Drop is one of my best," I said.

"But I'm not sure if I can learn all these," Amy whined, putting her pen down.

"Sure you can. Of course you won't learn them all at once. They take years to master. Why don't you try some of them tomorrow?" I suggested.

"OK," she said. "I will."

The next morning at nine fifteen, Stephen pulled out a rubber band. Amy looked over at me. I gave her a wink and a thumbs-up. She walked right over to Stephen and raised her eyebrows. I looked at the clock. She held them up for seven seconds. She looked like she just had a bad face-lift, but seven seconds is great for one's first Raised Eyebrow.

When she lowered her brows, Stephen said, "I did it."

"What?" asked Amy.

"My homework," he said.

"I don't want your homework."

"Then why are you looking at me like that?" Stephen asked.

"I want you to put the rubber band away," said Amy.

He put it away. Amy looked over at me. She looked sad.

I stood up and walked over to her.

"Don't worry," I said. "You'll get it. Like I said, it takes years of practice."

# Off with a Bang

*I have a good friend* named Troy. He is not a teacher. Troy works in a cubicle and types on his computer. Troy sits in a grown-up chair that is padded and has wheels. He does not have a ball box. He eats his lunch in a restaurant. Every once in a while Troy likes to tease me that my job is cushy.

"You get so much time off," he always says. "Two and a half months in the summer. Two weeks at Christmas. Spring break."

"Yes," I reply. "That's true. But teachers need time to recharge."

"Recharge?" he asked. "For what?"

I stared at him.

"For what?" I screamed. "Listen, you make a list of everything you do at work in one day. No, for one hour. And I'll make a list of everything I do in an hour, and we'll compare. OK?"

He agreed. So the next day, I began to record everything that happened in class. I started taking notes at 8:30 just as the kids walked in. Here's what I wrote:

Ryan told me he had to leave early for a dentist appointment, Matthew asked to use the bathroom, I started taking attendance, Ronny handed me a note from his mom, Aaron told me about his sleepover, and Michael asked what was for lunch.

Katie ran in late, Kevin gave me a picture he drew of Spider-Man, Peter said he didn't feel good, Aaron asked to borrow lunch money, Amanda asked me how to spell *octopus,* Natalie showed me her new Girl Scout patch, I picked up a glove off the floor, Kenny showed me how he could write "HELLO" on the calculator when you turn it upside down, I ordered three boxes of Girl Scout cookies from Melissa, and Melanie ran in with a frog.

Everyone ran over to Melanie, Tomoya asked to get a drink, I felt Peter's forehead, Ji Soo made fun of Katie's new haircut, I began collecting their homework, Joshua asked if I'd seen his sweater, I handed Aaron a dollar for lunch, Matthew wanted me to read his story, and I taped Spider-Man on the file cabinet.

Katie started crying, I sent Peter to the nurse, Joshua went to the lost and found to find his sweater, I refilled the tape dispenser and finished taking roll, Amanda announced that her dad is mad at her mom for leaving the car lights on, I pretended to read Matthew's story, Ji Soo apologized to Katie, I told Matthew his story was wonderful, and Ryan told me it was time for him to leave for the dentist.

I stopped writing at 8:47.

Later I showed Troy my list. He showed me his. Between 8:30 and 8:47, he waited at the coffee machine for his latte.

I'm not complaining. Really. I like frogs. I like Spider-Man. I like Girl Scout cookies.

There are those days, however, when I just don't want to stare at braces or look at new pierced ears or pick up sunflower shells. There are days when I just do not want to button up thirty-two raincoats and put on thirty-two pairs of gloves and hats and snow boots and then take them all off ten minutes later when the kids come back in from recess.

On these days I know it is time for me to go see my doctor. His name is Dr. Green. He is a miracle worker. One day with Dr. Green, and I'm back to my old self—ready for showbiz.

Oh, and if Dr. Green is unavailable, I schedule an appointment with one of his colleagues. Their names are Dr. Pool and Dr. Beach.

# Interview Questions

*The other day* I was thinking about the time when I interviewed for my very first teaching job. It's hard to believe that it has been twenty years.

I can still remember my first interview questions: What is your philosophy of education? What is your classroom management system? What is your discipline plan?

God if I knew.

This was my first interview. How in the world was I supposed to have an educational philosophy? I didn't even know what that meant.

So I made up my answers and tried to sound like I knew something. I guess I fooled them pretty well. I got the job, and they haven't fired me yet.

I still remember my responses to those first interview questions too. Boy, would my answers be different today, if I were asked those same questions.

Here's what I said then and what I'd say now:

**Question 1:** If I walked into your classroom, what would I see?
**Answer at first interview:** You would see children working col-

laboratively in peace and harmony, praising each other, and sharing their supplies happily with one another. You would see children thinking critically, helping their classmates, and encouraging one another.

**Answer today:** You'd see Brian hiding the soccer ball between his feet, Peter connecting markers together to make a really long one, and me looking for my coffee mug.

**Question 2:** What are your strengths?
**Answer at first interview:** I'm energetic and enthusiastic and extremely hardworking.
**Answer today:** I can pull off a Band-Aid so it won't hurt.

**Question 3:** What are your weaknesses?
**Answer at first interview:** I need to learn to not work so late at night and on the weekends and on all my holidays too.
**Answer today:** I steal apples off kids' cafeteria trays when I'm hungry.

**Question 4:** What is your philosophy of discipline?
**Answer at first interview:** I believe in giving children lots of positive reinforcement, and praising and encouraging students throughout the day, always working to build their self-esteem.
**Answer today:** Take away recess.

**Question 5:** What would you do with a difficult parent?
**Answer at first interview:** I would call the parent and listen to

her suggestions. I would work closely with her because we are a team, working together for the success of the child.

**Answer today:** Say, "Get a life."

**Question 6:** What would you do if a child threw a chair at you across the room?

**Answer at first interview:** First I would make sure that all the other children are safe. Then I would try to calm the student down. Next I would talk with the student and try to figure out what was bothering him, and help him explore his feelings. Together we would set up a behavior modification contract in which I would allow the child to set his own goals and choose his own rewards.

**Answer today:** Throw it back.

**Question 7:** What is a teacher's most important tool?

**Answer at first interview:** Love.

**Answer today:** Candy.

**Question 8:** What would your PE program look like?

**Answer at first interview:** Children would have the opportunity to develop multiple skills through a variety of individual and team sports where good sportsmanship is emphasized in a non-competitive environment.

**Answer today:** Heads up seven-up.

**Question 9:** How would you meet the individual differences of your students?

**Answer at first interview:** I believe in giving students a variety of choices. For example, when the children are practicing their spelling, the more visual child could draw pictures of her spelling words with different colored pens. The more kinesthetic child could write his words in sand or Jell-O pudding or ketchup or shaving cream.

**Answer today:** I believe in giving students a variety of choices. You can do your spelling now or you can do it at lunch.

**Question 10:** What is your view of constructivist education?

**Answer at first interview:** I think it is great. I think it is fantastic. I believe in it wholeheartedly. Is there any other way to teach?

**Answer today:** What the hell is that?

**Question 11:** Where do you see yourself in five years?

**Answer at first interview:** Teaching at your school and working toward a masters in education and participating in curriculum review and leadership training, and organizing the school's fund-raisers and selling wrapping paper for the band.

**Answer today:** Under an oak tree in Heavenly Gardens.

**Question 12:** Why should we hire you?

**Answer at first interview:** I like kids.

**Answer today:** I like kids.

# A Cultural Experience

*Every December* our school participates in Arts in Education Week. The county pays for students to attend various cultural events. This year I signed up to take my kids to see *The Nutcracker* at the civic center. Most of my students had never seen a ballet before. It would be a wonderful cultural experience for all of them.

And this trip would be extra special for my class because my friend, Tim, was performing in the ballet. Tim invited us all to come backstage after the performance.

Before we left, I gave speech 237.

"Got it?" I asked everyone.

"Got it!" they all answered in unison.

I assigned the kids to their cars, passed out maps to the mom drivers, and made sure Stephen went to the bathroom.

Soon we all piled into the cars and we were off.

I overheard Stephen and Ronny talking in the back seat.

"How come we're always in Mr. Done's car?" Stephen asked.

"'Cause we're his favorites," Ronny said.

I smiled.

About twenty songs and thirty-seven games of Find the Out-of-State License Plate later, we arrived at the theater. Hundreds of students from all over the county were there to see the ballet. We had great seats—fifth row orchestra.

If you've ever seen *The Nutcracker,* you remember the part of Mother Ginger. Mother Ginger wears an enormous hoop skirt. She walks out, lifts up her apron, and out skip dozens of little gingerbread children. When I was growing up, this was always one of my favorite parts.

Because of the weight of her skirt, the part of Mother Ginger is traditionally played by a man. And today Tim was playing the part of Mother Ginger.

My students sat enthralled through the whole performance. About halfway through the ballet, Tim walked out wearing the enormous skirt and a high, funny wig.

He walked around the stage, lifted up his apron, and out ran a dozen or more gingerbread children. They all ran around the skirt a couple of times and Tim lifted his apron once again. A few of the children hesitated before scurrying under the apron. It looked as if some did not want to go back inside.

After the performance, we all went backstage to see Tim. The kids were excited to meet Mother Ginger. I asked Tim if something went wrong with the gingerbread children.

"Oh, you noticed, huh?" He laughed.

Then he explained what had happened.

Apparently the cute little gingerbread children had been horrid little gingerbread children during rehearsal. Throughout the rehearsals, they had pulled the hair on Tim's legs, hit him, kicked him, stomped on his feet, and pinched him. One little gingerbread boy had even bit him. He told them over and over to stop, but they continued to brutalize him through the entire rehearsal run. And of course he couldn't do anything about it, because once the costume was on, he couldn't see them.

Well, finally Tim had had enough. So he decided to get back at them in that day's performance. Before the show, he ate three big bowls of chili. As soon as all the kids were under the apron and Tim was out on stage, he let go.

"They were trapped!" Tim laughed. "They could not escape till I lifted up the apron."

The kids all laughed.

"Thank you for telling us that story, Tim," I said sarcastically. "You want to ride back to school with these kids as they reenact the Mother Ginger scene?"

He laughed.

We all said good-bye to Tim, and as I expected, I spent the rest of the afternoon back at school telling Anthony and Carlos to stop making Mother Ginger noises with their hands under their armpits.

Actually, I was a bit worried to send the kids home that day. I could just hear the conversations around the dinner table that night.

"How was your visit to *The Nutcracker*, dear?" Anthony's mom would surely ask.

"Great!"

"What was your favorite part?"

"The part when Mother Ginger farted!"

So much for a wonderful cultural experience.

# Sugar Cookies

*Guess who* tore his kitchen apart this morning trying to find cookie cutters because today he was going to make sugar cookies with his students.

Guess who got all the way to school before he realized that he left the cookie cutters on the kitchen counter—along with the sugar and the butter and the eggs and the mixing bowl—and had to drive back home.

Guess which road was getting all its power lines fixed and all its traffic lights repaired and all its crosswalks painted and all its lanes widened this morning.

Guess who baked two frying pans in the staff room oven because he forgot to check the inside when he preheated it.

Guess whose student brought in a fancy new portable mixer for cookie making and lifted it out of the bowl while the beaters were still spinning at full speed.

Guess who couldn't find the off switch on his student's fancy new portable mixer.

Guess who was covered in cookie dough when the principal walked in.

Guess how many kids were running around the room trying to get away from the new fancy portable mixer when the principal introduced the new board members.

Guess what the first word was that the new board members heard out of the teacher's mouth.

# ER

*The other day* I walked out to the front of the school and checked the sign on the front of the building. It said, "School." I guess I really was in the right place. I thought maybe I had driven to the hospital by mistake.

You see, by the end of the day, I had held two bloody noses, wrapped a popsicle stick under a swollen finger, taken out a splinter, examined a bee sting, confiscated a pair of crutches, sent a kid home with a tummy ache, put on two Band-Aids, tightened an Ace bandage, signed a cast, and cleaned up after Ronny stabbed the ice pack with his scissors to see what was inside.

And that wasn't all. At the end of lunch, I saw Patrick sitting in the office. I walked over to him and put my hand on his head.

"Hey, Patrick. What's wrong?" I asked.

He looked up at me.

"I have to go home," he said.

"Why?" I asked.

"I have head lice."

I ran to the bathroom.

Some kids are accidents waiting to happen. Take James, for example. James is not allowed to change Penelope's water. In fact, James is not allowed near the sink. I don't know why, but for some reason James likes to stick his finger up the faucet. About once a month I have to call the custodian and have him come down and grease James's finger. Once we couldn't get his finger out, so we sent him home with the faucet.

Kevin is on prepaid lunch. Actually, he is not allowed to have any more money at school. Kevin likes to stick coins up his nose. I've become pretty good at dislodging the coins. Dimes and pennies are a cinch. Nickels are a bit more difficult. Once, though, we had to take Kevin to the hospital. He had found a quarter.

Winter is a busy season here at school. This December Emily came running into my classroom at lunch screaming, "Mr. Done! Mr. Done!"

"What's wrong, Emily?" I asked.

"Justin's stuck."

"Where is he?"

"On the monkey bars," she said. "Hurry!"

I walked to the staff room, got some hot water, and walked out to the blacktop.

"OK, everyone," I shouted. "Move aside."

There was Justin, stuck to the monkey bars again.

"Justin, how many times have I told you not to lick the monkey bars?" I asked.

"Ji Thoo ma-me," he said.

So I gave Speech 38: "And if Stephen told you to jump off a bridge, would you do that too?"

Last month Brian was playing on the monkey bars and fell off. He hurt his arm. It didn't look too bad, but we decided it was probably a good idea to have a doctor look at it. We tried to call Brian's parents, but couldn't get ahold of them. So Cathy covered my class and I drove Brian to the doctor's. I stayed in the waiting room while the doctor examined his arm. All of a sudden, Brian started screaming.

Gosh, I thought to myself, it's worse than I thought. In a couple of minutes, the doctor came out to the waiting room. I stood up.

"I didn't realize it was that bad," I said to the doctor. "I'm glad we brought him in."

"Oh, he'll be fine," said the doctor. "It's not broken."

"It's not broken? But it sounded awful. Why was he screaming so much?" I asked.

"Oh, we had to cut his Tommy Hilfiger shirt."

# The Christmas Concert

*I'll admit it.* I get choked up at Christmas concerts . . . I mean holiday concerts . . . I mean winter concerts . . . I mean solstice celebrations. What *are* we calling them these days?

Seeing my kids in outgrown suits and new party dresses and clip-on ties and white tights and green turtlenecks and little red vests always gets me. There is something truly magical about seeing hundreds of children standing on risers looking for their moms while singing Christmas carols in dress-up clothes to a full auditorium in December.

Our holiday concerts are always packed with moms and strollers, and dads and video cameras. There is always a steady stream of camera flashes. And every year the beginning band runs away with "Jingle Bells," and Mrs. Fisher tries to catch them. The band always wins.

This year after my group of kids sang, my job was to keep the strollers and the tripods and the little brothers and sisters out of the aisles so Justin could make his entrance at the end of the concert and say, "Ho! Ho! Ho!" Before he came on, I broke up three relay races, confiscated two paper airplanes, and caught a two-year-old just before he jumped up on stage and joined the choir.

The little boy next to me was standing on his mom's lap and

talking through the whole concert. I looked over a few times and hoped that the mom would take her child outside. She didn't. Finally I got up and stood in the back. I thought to myself, Times have changed. My mom would have taken me outside immediately if I were making a lot of noise. She spent many a Sunday listening to the church service from the crying room.

Then I spotted Mrs. Lee. She was there to see Nicole. Mrs. Lee sat with her two youngest boys: Gavin, a first grader, and Mason, who is in kindergarten. The boys were seated quietly on either side of her. Neither was standing on his seat or screaming or talking or crying or running down the aisle or throwing paper airplanes. Joy to the world! I started humming the "Hallelujah Chorus." The lady next to me tapped me on the shoulder and gave me the Raised Eyebrow.

# Sore Lips

*Some days* my back is sore from leaning over desks to fix pencil grips and make cursive *G*s. Some days my arms are sore from pitching in kickball and turning the jump rope seven million times at lunch. Some days my feet are sore from running bases in dress shoes. And some days my lips are sore too.

Once Emily came running into the classroom at recess.

"What's wrong, Emily?" I asked.

"Carlos said the *S-H* word!" she screamed.

"He did?" I asked.

"Uh-huh," she said, still out of breath.

"Well, what did he say?"

"I can't say it. My mom told me not to."

"OK, spell it for me. It's OK to spell it," I told her.

She spelled it out slowly. *"S-H-U-T."*

I leaned forward.

"Are you sure that's how you spell it?" I asked.

"Uh-huh," she answered.

"Are you sure it doesn't have an *I* in it?"

"I'm sure," she said.

"Tell me the word, Emily. I give you permission to say it."

She swallowed hard, then whispered, "Shut up."

I stared at her.

"He said 'shut up'?" I asked.

"Yes!" she nodded solemnly.

"Thank you for telling me, Emily. I'll take care of it. You may go outside now."

She did not see me bite my lip.

One Monday morning I asked James what he had done on the weekend.

"I went to the zoo," he replied.

"That's nice," I said. "What was your favorite animal?"

"The chicken with the Christmas tree that comes out of it," answered James.

"Huh?"

"The chicken with the Christmas tree," he said again.

I could not for the life of me figure out what he meant.

"You know," said James. And he plopped down on his knees and put his arms out like a fan.

"Oh." I smiled. "That's a peacock."

I covered my mouth. He did not see me bite my lip either.

I'm not the only one who gets sore lips. My colleagues do too. One day Kim, Dawn, and I were sitting in my classroom after school.

"You guys know my little Adam, right?" Kim asked.

"Yeah," we both answered.

"Well," said Kim. "Yesterday I asked the kids what they

wanted for Christmas, and Adam said he wanted to buy his mom and dad a new bed."

"A bed?" Dawn asked.

"Yes, a bed. So I asked him, 'Adam, why do you want to buy your mom and dad a new bed?' And you know what he said?"

She paused.

"He said, 'Because every night it makes a lot of noise. It must be broken.' "

Kim's lips were still hurting.

# Nicknames

*This week* we had our staff holiday party. Amy came too. As usual, the teachers started talking about work and our students. Amy was surprised.

"You guys talk about your students away from school?" she asked.

"All the time," I said.

It's true. Teachers talk about their students a lot. At parties. At home. In the car. Even on vacation, God forbid. And sometimes we give them nicknames.

Take Kung Fu, for example. I've forgotten what his real name was. Kung Fu sat at his desk and practiced karate chops all day long. This he did, of course, when he wasn't somewhere else in the room practicing his kicks.

If I ever needed anything, I went to see Simon. Simon never returned anything he borrowed. Ever. One day I made him clean out his desk. He found seven rulers, four bottles of Wite-Out, three protractors, nine pencil sharpeners, six dollars in change, two dictionaries, and seventeen pencils. I named him Wal-Mart.

Maker Upper rode on the killer whale at SeaWorld, went skydiving without a parachute, had an elevator in her bedroom, traveled to Zimbabwe, read *Harry Potter V* in one hour, owned a pet rhinoceros, and had been adopted three times.

Seung Jo thought "Line up!" meant "Let's play chase." And he thought that "Come here now!" meant "Run faster!" Sometimes I called him Hide-and-Seek. But most of the time I called him Catch Me If You Can.

Remember Nelly on *Little House on the Prairie?* I had her too. Her real name was Patty, but Nelly stuck. Nelly didn't like math, so she didn't do it. Nelly didn't like homework, so she didn't do that either. Nelly liked to complain and whine and pout. I purposefully did not put Nelly by the window. I was afraid I'd throw her out of it.

Some of this year's kids have already earned nicknames.

I call Anthony "Fiddles" because he cannot hold a paper clip without straightening it, has never touched a ruler without snapping it, and has never held an eraser without poking holes in it with his pencil.

Stephen's nickname is Demolition Derby. He has already taken apart three calculators, broken two yardsticks, carved his name into his chair, and eaten half a dozen pencils. You know those plastic bird stickers they put on windows to keep birds from flying into them? Well, we had to put Stephen's school photo on the sliding glass door at school to keep him from crashing into it.

Katie has the largest collection of empty juice boxes ever amassed by a third grader, and she saves the little holes that come out of the hole punch. I call her Smith, short for Smithsonian.

She spends half the day pulling stuff out of the trash can, and her favorite words are "Can I have this?" When I'm at school, I don't dare throw away anything that the kids have made for me because inevitably Katie will find it and bring it to me with a horrified look, and I have to lie and say the cleaning ladies must have accidentally thrown it away.

Emily is Barbara Walters. She gives me the regular updates every fifteen minutes on the behavior of everyone else in the class. "Mr. Done, Joey is not working. Mr. Done, Kevin is not reading. Mr. Done, Sean is eating the Legos. Mr. Done, you're sweating under your arms again."

Ryan can put his earlobes inside his ears, balance a pen between his upper lip and his nose, spin a ruler on the tip of a pencil, lean way back on the back two legs of his chair without falling over, and twirl two rolls of masking tape on his ears like hula hoops. He can of course perform all five feats for you at the same time, if you'd like him to. I call him Houdini.

Ronny's name is Trump. I swear he will be a millionaire by the time he is twelve. Before he leaves the classroom, I literally have to frisk him to make sure that he doesn't take any of his work outside with him. Last month he made twenty-seven dollars selling his drawings to the first graders. He says that someday he will be famous, and look what happened to Van Gogh.

And once I misplaced my car keys and offered a reward of a quarter to whoever found them. Well, Ronny found them. But then I kept losing my car keys about once a week, and every time I offered a reward, guess who kept finding my keys.

(I think he made about three dollars off me before I finally caught on.)

The week before Thanksgiving, Ronny went door-to-door selling Mrs. Hanson's Homemade Pumpkin Pies for $12.99 a piece, then went home and gave his mom the order for seventeen pies. She made him return the money.

But of all the students I've ever had, I think the one I will remember most is from my first year of teaching. Her name was Sally Carpenter. Sally was eight. She was the Drama Queen.

Once, we all walked into my classroom after PE. We had been playing kickball out in the field.

"Where's Sally?" I asked the rest of the class.

"She's out on the field," one of them answered.

"What?" I asked.

I walked outside and there she was, lying on the grass motionless.

"Sally!" I yelled.

No answer.

I shouted again. "Sally!"

Again, no answer.

I walked over to her.

Her eyes were closed. She was holding her breath.

"Sally Carpenter," I said firmly, "I know you are not dead. Get up this instant!"

No movement.

I began to count, "Oooone, Twwwwo . . ."

The corpse began to move. She stood up slowly. Her eyes were still closed.

"What happened?" I asked.

"I got sunstroke," she said, laying her hand on her head.

"It's cloudy. Now get inside."

About once a week after recess, the teacher on yard duty would poke her head in my door and say, "She's dead again." I would just continue my lesson till the door would open very slowly and Sally Sunstroke (she had several nicknames) would stagger into the room and flop herself onto her desk.

One day I was teaching the children some vocabulary words before we read our new story.

"Does anyone know what the word *desperate* means?" I asked.

Sally raised her hand. I was surprised. Usually no one knows that word.

"Sally, you know what *desperate* means?" I asked.

"Yes," she answered proudly.

"Can you use it in a sentence?" I asked.

"Of course," she replied.

Then Sally sat up on the edge of her seat, raised her chin, and announced, "Cleopatra was so desperate for Marc Anthony that she ripped all of her clothes off!"

I stared at her.

"Uh . . . thank you, Sally."

We used to have a program at our school called Kids Can

Write. All the third, fourth, fifth, and sixth graders in the whole district wrote stories, and a group of teachers met to score the papers. All the papers were mixed so we could not tell what grade the students were in. Nor could we see the names on the papers. We were to give each story a score of one through five. Five was the highest. So for the whole day a group of us sat reading stories and talking about the papers.

There was one story that moved everyone to tears. It was called "Bobo." I will never forget it. It was about a leopard in the wild jungles of South America trying to survive the hunters. It was a gripping story—certainly one of the best of the day, and one of only a few papers to receive a score of five. Nobody knew who had written it.

But I did. There was no mistaking *that* handwriting. Large. Flourishing. Dramatic. Slightly sunstroked.

Sometimes I wonder whatever happened to the Drama Queen. I keep waiting to see if she shows up on the Oscars or the Emmys. And I saved the "Bobo" story of course, just in case Sally is famous one day and I can sell her story to *People* magazine.

# Thank You!

*During the last week* before winter break some students bring in gifts for their teachers. It is very sweet. Sometimes you'll find a gift mysteriously placed on your desk at recess. Sometimes they'll hand it to you and say, "My mom told me to give you this. I don't know what it is." And sometimes the gifts come wrapped with lots of love and masking tape. Those are my favorites.

I try to wait till vacation to open my presents, but my students always beg me to unwrap them. And so I usually spend the last period of the year opening gifts in the corner of the room while thirty-two kids wait anxiously to see what I got.

"Thank you for the tie clip you made in your Easy-Bake Oven. I can't wait to wear it."

"Thank you for the orange Kleenex box cover. I like how you wrote your name so big with purple glitter glue."

"Thank you for the mug with your school photo on it. I see you right there."

"Thank you for the origami cranes. Are there really a hundred and fifty of them?"

"Thank you for the napkin holder you made at Cub Scouts. I didn't know you could make napkin holders out of nails."

"Thank you for the reindeer pin. Did you make it out of a clothespin? How clever. Oh, you want me to wear it now?"

"Thank you for the safety pin and paper clip ornament. Where did you buy it? Oh, you *made* it? Wow! I thought for sure you bought it!"

"Thank you for the T-shirt with your soccer team photo. And look, your whole team signed it."

"Thank you for the red, white, and blue plastic key chain. You braided it at Y-Camp? How did you know I needed a key chain?"

"Thank you for the sugar cookies. They look so yummy. And look at all those sprinkles and M&M's too. I can't wait to eat them."

"Thank you for the coaster. You got it in Las Vegas?"

"Thank you for the pot holder. What's that? . . . Your mom got it at her office party this year?"

"Thank you for the beautiful card. I love how you covered it with stickers. Oh my, did you cut out all this confetti?"

"Thank you for the pink and green candle you dipped over one hundred times on your visit to Williamsburg. It's beautiful."

"Thank you for the scarf. It's so nice. Do you know where your mom bought it? Is the receipt in the box?"

"Ohh . . . thank you. It's beautiful. I love it. You made it? . . . Can you tell me about it? . . . Of course it's a paperweight! Oh, it's a beautiful paperweight. Thank you so much for the paperweight. Look everyone, it's a paperweight. See?"

"Thank you for the Santa boxer shorts. They're from your mother? . . . Uh . . . how . . . colorful. Thank you. Tell your mom . . . uh . . . Merry Christmas."

# How to Know When
# You Need a Vacation

*When you can't remember* the name of the student who has been sitting in front of you for the last sixty-seven days.

When you drive away from the coin-op car wash and don't realize that your car is still covered with soapsuds.

When you spend five minutes trying to turn off the TV with your cell phone.

When you leave the mall after Christmas shopping to find that your car has been stolen from the parking garage, and you go home and call your insurance company, and the next day Sears calls to tell you that they have finished rotating your tires, and when will you come in to pick up your car?

When you can't remember how to spell "PE."

When your Secret Santa gives you Extra Strength Tylenol and you are thrilled.

When you welcome all the parents in the cafeteria to the big Winter Concert, and sit down at the piano and begin playing the first song, and suddenly realize that you forgot to get the 120 children who are still waiting for you to pick them up in the library.

When you run around school for thirty minutes looking for the coffee mug that is in your hand.

When you finish giving the spelling test, then turn around and see the entire spelling list still written on the board.

When you say, "OK, boys and girls, time to start tidying up," twenty minutes before the beginning of recess.

When you're reading *James and the Giant Peach* to the class and you use the exact same voice for James and Aunt Spiker and Aunt Sponge and the Centipede and the Grasshopper and the Ladybug too.

When you open all the doors on your advent calendar on the first day.

When you are upset because the *Charlie Brown Christmas* video is only twenty-seven minutes.

When it is three in the morning and you are humming "Frosty the Snowman" for the 157th time with your eyes wide open in bed.

# The First Day of Winter Break

*Over the years* I have become quite good at telling when a child will be sick. You see, germs are sequential. They tend to travel side to side. Seldom do they jump to the student behind or in front. And rarely do they skip rows.

This year Ronny sits next to Sarah, and Sarah sits next to Anthony. If Ronny is sick, I know that Sarah will be sick in a day or two. And when Sarah is out, I know that soon Anthony will be watching cartoons and eating popsicles at home.

One day Carlos asked me, "What are you doing, Mr. Done?"

"Getting your work folder ready for tomorrow," I answered.

"Why?" he asked.

"Because tomorrow you're going to be home," I replied.

He looked at me funny.

"Huh?" he asked.

"Here," I said, and I handed him the folder.

Sure enough, the next day he was out.

Two weeks before vacation, there was a really bad little bug making its way across row three. The kids were out for days. I thought I was safe. I was two rows away and I took every conceivable precaution. But this little bugger was a row jumper. And it landed on me—just in time for winter break.

On Saturday morning, the first day of vacation, I couldn't get out of bed. I could not breathe. I could not swallow. My head felt like someone had just sharpened it. I lay there thinking, This can*not* be happening to me!

Today was the day I was going to take my slacks into the dry cleaners to see if they could get the Elmer's glue out. Today I was going to clean the coffee mugs out of my car. Today I was going to finish writing all my thank-you cards for the mugs and ties and Old Spice. Today I was going to return all the mugs and ties and Old Spice.

Today I was going to telephone all my friends whom I have not spoken to for three weeks because of band rehearsals and toy drives and winter bazaars and wrapping paper sales and tell them that I am still alive.

Oh, I can*not* be sick. Not again. Not again this year. Why does this happen to me every December?

I was so careful this year too. I handed out Kleenex every morning when the kids walked through the door. I checked their foreheads every hour. I handed out vitamin C and said it was the newest M&M. I sent them to the nurse the second I detected a sniffle.

The nurse got mad at me. She sent me a note.

"Mr. Done, I have seven of your students in my office. What's going on?" she asked.

I wrote back, "They're hot."

She wrote another note: "Well, maybe you should let them

take their coats and hats and gloves off in class!" And she sent them all back.

"Hey!" I screamed. "Why are you guys back? You're sick! Get out of here!"

"The nurse said we're fine," Kenny said.

"But she asked if you were feeling all right," said Amanda.

For weeks I sang, "Wash your hands with soap," "Button your coats," "Put on your mittens," "Cover your mouths when you cough," and "Don't sneeze on me!"

I jumped back when they coughed. I ran away when they started to sneeze. I disinfected their pencils. I made them gargle with Listerine after lunch. I had three sick drills a day.

"OK, everyone," I ordered, "cover your mouths! Now cough! Good. Now, let's do it again."

Oh, why didn't they listen to me?

"I know Natalie did not want to miss the Christmas party, Mrs. Robertson, but she has a fever of a hundred and two!"

"Joshua, you have strep throat! What do you mean your mom has to get her hair done and can't find a sitter?"

Right now Stephen is probably sledding somewhere in perfect health while I sit here with a Vick's inhaler jammed up my nose. And Michael is probably playing computer games while I lie on the couch deciding what flowers I want at my funeral.

Oh, I am *so* glad my kiddies got well just in time to enjoy their hard-earned vacation. I am *so* happy that I didn't cough or sneeze or sniff on them and prevent any one of them from having a well-deserved holiday.

Next year this will *not* happen. Next year if I hear so much as a sniffle, I'm not letting any of them into the classroom without a note from the surgeon general. Next year I will teach in a mask. Next year we will sterilize all scissors, pencils, and rulers. And if they raise their hands for help, they'd better be wearing gloves!

# Jealous

*At the beginning* of each New Year, I always go out to lunch with my old friend Janis. Janis and I graduated from college at the same time. I was in the teacher education department. She was in business. Janis wanted to make money. I wanted to walk kids to the cafeteria.

Janis is a partner for some big finance firm with a lot of names in the title. I don't know what she does, really. Something with audits, I think. I don't even pretend to understand. The hardest math I teach is long division.

Janis just bought a summer house, flies to Monte Carlo for the weekend, and drives a BMW. I did not, cannot, and never will.

It really isn't fair, if you think about it. Janis and I both entered the workforce at the same time, and now she makes over twice what I do. Janis drives a nice company car and gets a nice big ten to fifteen percent raise and a hefty bonus every year. Her company is always flying her somewhere. For me, the only good thing about all this is that I make her pay for lunch.

Last week Janis had just returned from Berlin. She stayed in one of those big fancy-shmancy hotels where they put fruit baskets in your room and cottonballs in the bathroom. She was treated to cocktail parties and seven-course meals with snails and caviar, and went on moonlit boat trips at night.

"I'm jealous!" I screamed, slamming my hands on the table.

"Why?" she asked.

"Because the last time my school sent me anywhere, it was to the Elk's Lodge," I explained. "And we had to bring our own bag lunch. That's why! And you know something else? I have never had a cup of coffee without contributing to the coffee kitty. And I have never gone to a staff party without chipping in for the pizza."

She laughed.

"Who pays for all your trips and hotels and fruit baskets?" I asked.

"Oh, sometimes my company. But mostly the clients," she answered.

"Clients!" I screamed. "You know who my clients are? My clients don't eat the crust. My clients only drink chocolate milk. My clients will only eat something if there is a toy inside the box. My clients do not eat anything with nuts. And my clients would make loud gagging noises and fall down dead if I asked them if they wanted any caviar. Stop laughing!"

"OK, OK," she said. "But what if you want to go to a conference or something?" she asked.

"A conference?" I asked. "The only conferences I have are with parents who did not know their sweet little angels knew those four-letter words."

"No, seriously," she said.

I paused and leaned forward. "Janis," I said, "let me explain. If we want to go to a conference, we pay for it ourselves."

"Really?" she asked. "And how do you buy books and blocks, and all that stuff that you teachers use?"

I looked at her. "Janis, how much do you think teachers get each year to buy all that stuff?"

"I don't know."

"Come on. Take a guess," I said.

She thought about it. "I don't know. A couple thousand maybe."

"Take off a zero and you'll be close."

"You're kidding," she said.

"Let's just put it this way," I explained. "We get about as much a year as you just paid for the minibar in Berlin."

"No way!" she screamed.

"It's true." I continued, "And at least I've been teaching for a while. I've accumulated stuff. It's worse for the new teachers. They start out with nothing. Do you know what I got when I started teaching?"

"What?" she asked.

"A staple remover, a globe from 1939, and an ant farm," I explained. "I spent my whole first year picking staples out of the carpet and staring at ants."

"Oh, that reminds me," she said. Janis reached into her purse. "Here are the cottonballs you wanted."

"Thanks," I said.

The waiter placed our lunches on the table. I looked at her BLT.

"Say, can I have your toothpicks?" I asked.

She looked at her sandwich. "Sure. Why?"

"I can use them at school."

She laughed. "You want my straw too?"

"Sure," I said.

"I'm kidding."

"I'm not. Hand it over," I said, holding out my hand.

I smiled and stared at her salad. "Say, did I tell you we have a class bunny?" I said.

She covered her plate. "You are *not* taking my salad!"

# Letter to Roald Dahl

Dear Mr. Dahl,

I so enjoy reading your books to my students. Your books have brought hours of happiness to my classroom. Thank you so much. I am writing to ask you one small favor. If at all possible, would you mind, please, changing one little word in *Charlie and the Chocolate Factory?*

You see, every year I read *Charlie* to my students. Each child follows along in his or her own copy as I read it aloud. The children love the book. And so do I. Why, I have read it for twenty years, and I still love it. Yes, Mr. Dahl, everything is just grand. That is of course until we get to chapter 7.

At the end of chapter 6 I start to break out in a cold sweat. My voice starts to tremble because I know it is coming. Then I see it. I see the word that has ruined so many a reading hour. I try to skip over it quickly. I pray that no one will notice. But they always notice. In twenty years I have never had a student *not* notice. I ask you, Mr. Dahl, was it really necessary to write the word "ass"?

Do you know what it is like having a classroom full of third graders read that word? Do you? Let me explain what happens. First Michael jumps out of his seat and runs to show me. Then the rest of the class jumps out of their seats. They all run around the room laughing and pointing to that word.

Then Anthony keeps repeating the word. I scream, "Do not say that word!" Then some little wise guy asks, "What word?" trying to get *me* to say the word. Then I repeat, "Do not say that word!" Then another little smart aleck says, "But it's in the book!" This, Mr. Dahl, goes on for about ten minutes.

Then the begging begins. They beg me to reread the chapter so that they can jump out of their seats and run around the room and point to the word and laugh some more.

This year was one of the worst. Melanie said she's telling her mother that I swore in class. And Justin? Justin had to be rushed to the nurse's office for oxygen. Quite frankly, Mr. Dahl, I'm trying to have a nice reading hour, and you're *ruining* it!

Yours sincerely,

Mr. Done

# I Had a Dream

*On Monday morning* the children walked into the room and sat down.

"Good morning, boys and girls," I said. "I hope you all had a nice weekend. Oh, there will be no homework tonight. In fact, there will be no homework for the rest of the year."

They all cheered.

"What's wrong, Mr. Done?" asked Stephen.

"Yeah. Why are you being so nice?" Emily asked.

"Oh, no reason." I smiled. "No reason at all."

But there was a reason. You see, last night I had a dream.

I had a dream that I had to have a triple heart bypass, and right before they put me under, I looked up at my doctor, and it was Anthony.

I had a dream that I visited my financial planner the day after I retired, and it was Sarah.

I had a dream that I bought a house in Florida and the real estate agent was Katie.

I had a dream that I moved to a new house and my next door neighbor was Ronny.

I had a dream that I was flying to my fiftieth high school reunion and the pilot was Justin.

I had a dream that I had to have an emergency root canal and the oral surgeon was Stephen.

I had a dream that I got pulled over for speeding and the officer was Melanie.

I had a dream that the limousine picked me up for my niece's wedding and Natalie was the chauffeur.

I had a dream that I went to the chiropractor and it was Brian.

I had a dream that I was being audited by the IRS and the agent was Peter.

I had a dream that I finally went to see a therapist and it was Emily.

"Anyone want any candy?" I asked.

"Yeah!" they all screamed.

I started handing it out.

"Mr. Done, are you sure you're feeling OK?" Emily asked.

"Yes. Yes. I'm fine. Just fine, Emily. I just had a weird dream last night. That's all," I said.

She pulled up a chair and said, "Would you like to talk about it?"

# Tortilla Snowflakes

*When I was a kid,* I would only eat two things: Kraft macaroni and cheese, and pork and beans. That was it. So my mom's cupboards were always full of both. These were staples in my house.

Well, teachers have their staples too. Teacher staples are those tried-and-true activities that you can pull out at any time and know, like the pork and beans, the kids will love them.

One of my favorite teaching staples is making paper snowflakes. You know the kind I mean—the ones where you take a piece of white paper, fold it, cut out shapes, and open it back up. A recent study of 100,000 teachers found that making paper snowflakes is the one thing that all elementary school teachers have in common.

Well, one day I pulled out the white paper and scissors. As they began cutting their paper snowflakes, I announced, "Boys and girls, today we are going to make snowflakes that you can eat!"

"Yeah!" everyone screamed.

Edible snowflakes are similar to paper ones, but instead of paper, you use flour tortillas. You fold the tortillas, cut out shapes, open them up, and ta-da! Tortilla snowflakes. Fried in a little butter and topped with powdered sugar, they're yummy. Kids love them.

Well, as the kids were cutting out their tortillas, I put some butter into a skillet, laid Natalie's tortilla into the pan, and placed the pan on a single burner I borrowed from the science room. Then I went over to help Anthony cut his tortilla.

All of a sudden Natalie screamed, "Mr. Done! Look!"

I turned back around. Natalie's snowflake was smoking. I ran to the burner, pulled the pan off, and ran to the window. Just as I was opening the window, the fire alarm went off.

I put my hand on my head and said a bad word under my breath.

"Mr. Done, the fire alarm!" Melissa screamed.

"Mr. Done, the fire alarm!" Joey yelled.

"Mr. Done, the fire alarm!" Sean shouted.

"OK, everyone, let's go outside," I said.

Emily grabbed her coat and Melanie grabbed Penel. We lined up and walked outside. In the hall we met Mike's class.

"Hey, who was the dummy who set off the fire alarm?" asked Mike.

"I heard they set it off in the cafeteria," I said.

Peter began to explain, "Mr. Done, you—"

I covered Peter's mouth quickly. I did not want him to inhale any smoke.

Outside we lined up in the parking lot with 650 other students and teachers. It was raining.

Cathy came running over to me.

"What happened?" she asked.

I looked around for Amy. I did not see her.

"Uh . . . well," I said, "Amy was cooking in class, and set off the smoke detector. Poor Amy," I said. "She must be so embarrassed."

Finally the bell rang and we all went back inside. We got back to the room and I sent the kids to lunch. I clicked on my computer.

Note: Never check your e-mails immediately after you have just set off the fire alarm and sent 650 students and their teachers outside into the rain.

Marion wrote, "My kids thank you. They got out of a spelling test today."

Kim wrote, "I'd like mine extra crispy also please."

Dawn wrote, "Join the club."

There were about fifteen more e-mails, but I chose not to read them. Instead I clicked off the computer and called my mom.

"Hi, Mom," I said. "Can I come over for dinner tonight?"

"Sure. Anything particular you want?"

"Yeah. Macaroni and cheese."

# Valentine's Art

***Once on Valentine's Day*** I wrote "LOVE" in giant letters on six different pieces of large white paper.

"OK, boys and girls," I said. "Today we're going to decorate the letters. You may decorate them any way you'd like."

I placed the letters on the floor and handed out crayons and markers and colored pencils. The kids sat around the giant letters and began to color away.

About ten minutes later in walked Mr. Anderson, the superintendent, with a group of about five or six men in suits and ties. I think they were other principals. They looked important. Mr. Anderson was giving them a tour of the school.

The men stood around the kids and watched them color. Tomoya was coloring in the *L* with rainbows. James drew happy faces in the *O*. Jenny was drawing big red polka dots in the *V*, and Erika was lying on her tummy, quite intent on filling in her *E* with hearts and arrows.

Mr. Anderson knelt down next to Erika.

"What are you doing there, honey?" Mr. Anderson asked.

Erika looked up from her work with an isn't-it-obvious sort of look on her face and sighed.

"Can't you see we're making love?" she said.

Mr. Anderson's face turned red. The other men turned away. Erika went back to work.

# Spring

# Spring Is Here

*When do you know* spring has arrived? When Safeway puts out their Easter candy? When we go on daylight savings time? When the drugstore starts selling kites?

I know spring is here when I hear the first song flute. Mrs. Fisher always passes out the song flutes the first week of March. She has done so for the past twenty years.

Come March, third graders in my school are everywhere practicing "Mary Had a Little Lamb," "Row, Row, Row Your Boat," and "Jingle Bells." On the blacktop. In the hall. In the cafeteria. Everywhere I go, it's "Mr. Done, listen to this! Listen to this!"

One day before school I met three of my boys in the hallway. They were sitting in their cubbies playing "Three Blind Mice."

"Stop playing that song!" I yelled. "I have heard it three hundred times this week. Play something else!"

"That's all we know," said Peter.

"Well, that's *enough!* Now go play outside!" I yelled.

I went into the staff room and poured the last bit of coffee into my World's Greatest Teacher mug. Then I walked into the faculty bathroom, opened a stall door, and sat down. It's my hideout.

All of a sudden, I heard music coming from the next stall.

"Who's in there?" I screamed.

No answer.

"You heard me. Who's in there?" I asked again.

"Me," a voice answered quietly.

"Peter!" I yelled, "I told you to go play!"

"I am," Peter said.

"I meant outside! Is Carlos in there too?" I asked.

No answer.

"Carlos?" I said slowly.

"Yeah," Carlos mumbled.

"Anthony, are you in there too?" I asked.

"Yeah," said Anthony.

"Aha! The third mouse."

"Mr. Done, listen to this echo," said Peter.

He started playing. I sang along.

"Three bad boys. Three bad boys. See how they run. See how they run. They did not listen to Mr. Done. So their mommies came over and took them home. See how they run. See . . ."

The stall door opened. There was a scampering of feet. I stayed and drank my coffee.

A couple of minutes later, two more mice crept into the bathroom. I recognized their voices. They did not know I was having my morning coffee. I sat silent.

"Are you sure we can play in here?" Justin whispered.

"Yeah," said Brian. "Come on. It echoes really good."

They walked into the stall next to mine, closed the door, and began to play their song flutes. I waited a minute, then I howled as loud as I could. Both boys screamed and ran out of the bathroom. I think I gave Justin a heart attack.

I laughed to myself and finished my coffee.

. . . How do I know spring has arrived?

When the song flute monster appears.

# Testing

*Thirty-two sharpened* number two pencils and a stack of practice tests just arrived in my box. I looked through the tests. Fractions. Decimals. Time. Geometry.

"Eek!" I said out loud. I hadn't taught any of this yet. Will someone please explain to me why we must have everything taught by March? Am I wrong, or aren't there three months left of school?

I gave a big sigh and walked into the classroom.

"Good morning, boys and girls," I said. "I'm afraid I have some bad news. I cannot read to you after lunch anymore. We cannot have any more discussions. I do not have time to look at your stitches or your mosquito bites or your tadpoles. We have to get ready for the test!"

I continued, "Today we are going to learn how to find the area of a square, and the perimeter of a rectangle, and the volume of a cube, and prove the quadratic formula. Today we have to learn how to add, subtract, multiply, and divide fractions, and find main ideas and supporting details. Today we have to learn where to put periods and commas and question marks and quotation marks and semicolons."

"What's that?" Patrick asked.

"No time for questions, Patrick." And I continued, "Today we have to learn how to use the atlas and the thesaurus and the encyclopedia and the almanac. Today we have to improve your decoding levels by three years. That should take us up to morning recess."

The whole class groaned.

"You don't like these tests?" I asked. "You don't want to do these tests? Don't you realize that these scores are published in the newspaper and parents and real estate agents everywhere look at these scores? Don't you realize that your parents' property values are affected if you don't know how to find the diameter of a circle?"

"You want to paint?" I continued. "You want to run? You want to sing? You want to do a play? You want to go on a field trip? You want to play your song flute? Ha! What do you think this is? A school?"

I stood on my chair.

"Boys and girls," I proclaimed, "you must learn to fill in all the bubbles completely. You must learn to bubble in anything as fast as you can when the teacher shouts, 'Ten seconds left!' You must learn to make dark marks with your pencil so the Scantron machine can read your answer. You must learn to erase completely if you decide to change your answer. And you must learn to guess even if you don't know what bubbles to fill in. You must learn to answer fifty verbal ability questions, thirty vocabulary questions, forty-five reading comprehension questions, forty-five quantitative ability questions, and seventy-five math questions in fifteen minutes! Understand? Good. Now come on, everyone, let's get to work!"

Why do we continue to give these tests? I ask myself. And why are we placing more and more value on them every year? We know that they do not accurately measure what a child really knows. We know that they do not indicate how well a child is doing in school. We know that one of your best math students can fill in one wrong bubble on the answer sheet and get a zero out of ten in math.

One of these days I'm going to get my courage up. When the tests arrive in my mailbox, I'm just going to send them right back with a note saying, "Sorry. Can't do. We're looking at tadpoles today."

# April Fools!

*There are* hundreds of books on how to teach reading and how to teach math and how to manage your classroom and how to decorate your bulletin boards and how to motivate your students. But I have yet to see one book on how to get through April Fool's Day.

Each year thousands of first-year teachers walk blindly into their first April without any guidance on how to survive it. I feel sorry for them. The following is a list of rules on how to survive April first with thirty-two children including Stephen.

**RULE 1:** Call in sick.

**RULE 2:** Never eat anything handed to you by a student on the first of April, unless of course you like to eat Oreos filled with toothpaste.

**RULE 3:** Never drink anything handed to you by a student on April 1 either, unless you like drinking Pepto-Bismol or salt water in a 7-Up can.

**RULE 4:** Never go to the bathroom on April Fool's Day, unless you are good at detecting plastic wrap stretched under the toilet seat.

**RULE 5:** Play dumb.

But you cannot play dumb the same way for each trick. Certain tricks require different degrees of playing dumbness. For instance, when you see Stephen blowing up a Ziploc sandwich bag after lunch, pretend that you do not notice. When your students direct you to sit down on your chair, pretend that you do not know there is a Ziploc whoopee cushion under the sweater that has been placed on your chair. And pretend that you do not see them trying hard not to crack up as you prepare to sit in the chair. After you sit down, jump up and act surprised. When Stephen pulls out his lunch bag from under the sweater, look even more shocked and ask, "Who put that there?"

When Justin pats you on the back, pretend that you do not feel the Post-it note that he just put on your shirt. Then walk around the room so everyone can read the note. The more you walk around the room and pretend that you do not know there is a sticky note that says "Kick Me!" on your back, the more everyone will laugh. When the sticky note falls off, stop walking so that Justin can pick it up and put it back on your back.

When you see a plastic spider on your desk, jump away and scream. When you see the plastic snake on your chair, jump away and scream. And when you see the plastic dog poo on the floor, jump away and scream again. Act like you think they are real.

When the children fall over laughing after you discover the plastic poo, turn and stare at the children like you are horrified. Say nothing. Then turn and look back at the poo. Then turn and look at the students again. Then look at the dog poo again. The more you turn and look at the dog poo, then back at the students, the more they will laugh.

Oh, and don't forget to tell Stephen to put the plastic dog poo and snake and spider back into his backpack, or he will do it all over again five minutes later, and everyone will laugh as if they did not just see it five minutes ago.

Parents are lucky. They drop their little darlings off on April first with their backpacks full of salt water and plastic throw-up and drive away. I wonder. Did Stephen's mom think about what he would do with his new plastic toys?

This year I decided to get the parents back. At the end of the day, I wrote notes to each of the kids' parents. Each note said this:

Dear Parents,

Your child was fooling around in class today. He was very disruptive. He would not do his work, and he talked back all day long. Please speak with him.

Sincerely,
Mr. Done

After writing the notes, I turned each child's paper over and wrote, "April Fools!" in tiny letters on the bottom corner of each note. So just as the moms start to scream at their kids for misbehaving in school, the kids turn over the notes and shout, "April Fools!"

The parents would not expect to be April-fooled by the

teacher. The kids could hardly wait to go home and trick their parents.

The next day Stephen walked into class. He looked sad.

"What's wrong, Stephen?" I asked.

"I'm grounded for a month," he said.

"Why?"

"I showed my mom the note."

"And?" I asked.

"She got mad," Stephen said. "I turned over the note to show her what you wrote, but it was blank."

"Blank?"

"You forgot to write on the back of my paper," Stephen said.

I smiled. "April Fools!"

**RULE 6:** If you can't beat 'em, join 'em.

# The Wedding

*My first year of teaching,* Miguel brought in his camera to class.

"Mr. Done," he asked. "Can I take a picture of you?"

"Sure," I said. "Why?"

"I want to send it to my aunt," he said. "She needs a husband."

Any teacher who is single will tell you that your students will try to marry you off. Every year my class picks one woman in the school and decides that she should be my wife.

"You should marry Ms. Sanders," said Sarah.

"She's married!" I said.

That didn't matter of course. The only thing that mattered was that I was not.

"You should marry Ms. Carter," said Justin. "You can marry her. She's divorced."

Ms. Carter has been divorced for fifty years.

If I so much as speak to a woman at school, the kids think we are getting married: the secretary, the nurse, the crossing guard, the cafeteria lady, the noon supervisor, the principal. Even their own moms are candidates.

Whenever a teacher gets married, it is a big deal at school. This year my friend Lisa announced her engagement, and the whole school was buzzing. Cathy had a shower for the staff. The room moms threw a shower for Lisa in the cafeteria and invited all her students. The kids made all the decorations and presented Lisa with a book. It was entitled *When You Get Married.* It was full of advice from the children:

"When you get married, you must remember to take your ring off before you take a bath so you don't lose it."

"When you get married, you must remember to come back to school."

"When you get married, set the table."

And, "When you get married, you should call your husband nicknames like 'Dear,' and 'Honey,' and 'My Little Fish.' "

Lisa invited the whole staff to her wedding, and her whole class too. Most of her kids sat in the first few rows with their parents. But I don't know if it is such a good idea to invite your students to your wedding.

They threw birdseed like they were playing dodgeball. The candles in the reception hall were all blown out before the wedding party arrived. The frosting flowers were gone when it was time to cut the wedding cake. The Just Married sign was misspelled. And five of her boys dog-piled on the floor to catch her garter.

Actually, Lisa's kids were pretty well behaved at the ceremony, I must say. Well, that is, until the end of the service. Just as the groom lifted her veil and moved in to give Lisa a kiss, the entire front row screamed, "Yuck!"

# Believe Them

*Did you ever* wonder where the Boy Who Cried Wolf goes to school? He goes to mine. In fact, he is in my class. His name is Sean. Sean usually talks with his fingers crossed behind his back. And about once a week, he walks up to me and points to the sky, or my pants, or my shoes, and screams, "Mr. Done, *look!*" I look and Sean shouts, "You looked! You looked!" and laughs. It's the highlight of his week.

Some days, however, I refuse to look at my zipper that is supposedly down, or my shoelaces that are untied, or the UFO that has just landed on Miss Carlson's office. This drives Sean crazy.

The other day Sean hopped up to my desk.

"Mr. Done, I can't straighten my leg," he said.

I looked down at his leg. His right knee was bent. I gave him the Chin Down and told him to go back to his seat. He hopped back.

A few minutes later Sean came up to my desk again.

"Mr. Done, really, I can't make my leg straight," he said again.

"Sean Warren," I said (teachers use middle names just like parents do), "get back to work."

He shrugged his shoulders and hobbled back to his desk. I shook my head. What an actor, I thought to myself. But later that day as I was reffing an intense game of kickball, I noticed that Sean really was hobbling.

"Sean, come here," I yelled.

He hopped on over.

"Stand up straight," I said.

"I told you. I can't."

"Let me see it," I said, kneeling down.

I tried to straighten Sean's leg. It wouldn't straighten. I took him to the office, and the nurse called his mom. His mom took him to the hospital, and they X-rayed his leg. The doctor found a pin right behind his kneecap.

Apparently Sean had knelt on the carpet in class, and just as he knelt down, a pin slid right behind his kneecap. He didn't even feel it. He brought the pin to school the next day for show and tell.

Last week Sean walked up to my desk once again and said, "Mr. Done, I don't feel good."

"Show me your leg," I said.

"It's not my leg. It's my stomach," he said.

"You're fine. Go sit down."

We go through this same routine once a week. Always during math time. Sean walks up to my desk, says he is not feeling well, and I send him back to his seat.

Well, about five minutes later, Sean was back at my desk again. (We were doing decimals.)

"Mr. Done, I really don't feel well," he said again. "Can I go to the bathroom?"

"Sean, you're fine. Go do your math," I said.

He walked back to his chair. A couple of minutes later, he was up at my desk again.

"Sean! That's enough!" I shouted.

"But, Mr. Done," he said. "I—"

Then out it flew. All of it. His entire breakfast and lunch. Cap'n Crunch and sloppy joes. All over my desk. All over my shirt. All over my shoes. I wiped my clothes as best I could and taught the rest of the day in my socks.

# Parents

*Most parents are great.* They drive their vans on field trips and even volunteer to take the boys. They buy cookies from the Girl Scouts, candles from the Cub Scouts, and candy bars from the Retired Teachers Association. They collect plastic bottles and wash out aluminum cans for the new play structure and sew Uncle Sam vests and Glinda dresses the night before the school play.

But once in a while you get some real doozies. Fortunately, those times are rare. One year a friend of mine had a really rough group of parents. It got so bad that she finally put a sign outside her classroom door that said, "No dogs or parents allowed!"

They say that a teacher is doing well if he can please ninety percent of the parents. Here are the letters I never sent to the other ten percent.

Dear Mrs. Proud,

I know your son is not reading like some of the other children. He is a boy. He wants to play. Yes, he is not reading the same book as your neighbor's child, but he is reading. And he is progressing. Please, chill out.

Dear Mrs. Challenge,

You came in and said your child is not being challenged. It is the second week of school. I am still learning their names. Attached you will find her math test. As you can see, she missed half the problems. Could you please help your brain surgeon learn how to add? Thank you.

Dear Mr. Permissive,

You're shocked at your son's language at school? Your son watches MTV all day long. He has every rap song memorized. He has seen more R-rated movies than I have. Please turn off the television.

Dear Mrs. Uptight,

Yes, the bus for the field trip is safe. No, your son will not have to really kiss Snow White in the school play. Yes, I know he is allergic to peanuts, and I will not give him any for snack. Thank you for the water bottle; I will make sure he doesn't get dehydrated.

Dear Mrs. Maintenance,

I am sorry, but I do not have time to monitor your son's time-release medication every ten minutes and chart it on a graph as you requested.

Dear Mr. Pusher,

Please don't be upset about your son's B+ in math. No, this will not hurt his chances of getting into Stanford. No, he does not need a private math tutor now. And by the way, does he really need to take tennis and piano and swimming and karate and violin and polo lessons?

Dear Mrs. Stage Mom,

I received your lengthy e-mail about your daughter's not getting the lead in the school play. She has a very nice part, as all the children do, and I'm sure will have a wonderful experience. Sorry, I cannot go back and reaudition all the third grade girls as you would like.

Dear Mrs. Issues,

I was not discriminating by discussing slavery in my classroom. I was not favoring the boys when I had one more boy solo than girl solo in the school musical. I am not prejudiced because I happen to have more Asian students sitting on one side of the room than the other. If you asked me how many boys and girls or blacks or Asians or Hispanics I have, I could not tell you. They are children. I see children.

Dear Mr. Perfectionist,

Please do not do your child's work. I cannot help him if you write his papers for him. It is OK for him to make mistakes. Please let him. And please do not tell me that he did it all by himself when he didn't. I can tell. "Philanthropy" and "fundamental" and "significant" are not words that eight-year-olds use in their writing.

Dear Mr. Drill Sergeant,

I know you are trying to instill in him a sense of responsibility, but your son is only eight years old. He is not eighteen. He is eight. Yes, it would be nice if he were self-motivated and organized and sat down and did his homework by himself and remembered his backpack and his sweater and his lunch money. But he doesn't. He needs your help. He is eight.

Dear Mr. Blame,

I am sorry for calling you and telling you about your son's poor behavior at school. I thought you would want to know. I am sorry you think that it is my fault, and that I did something to provoke your darling little angel.

Dear Mrs. Weird,

Please do not drop by anymore in the middle of math and say that you just received a "psychic envelope" from Joey and you're sure that he needs to talk with you. The post office is closed today.

# French Lessons

*For years* I've wanted to learn how to speak French, so this year I finally started taking lessons. I began my lessons in September with a nice, little old French Canadian lady named Grace. Grace lives close to school. I drive over to her house every Wednesday after work for my lesson. We began with numbers and how to tell time.

It's not going as quickly as I had hoped. It's March, and I still don't know all my numbers, and when Grace asks me the time, I still point to my watch.

To help me study, I labeled everything in my house with sticky notes. It helps me remember the vocabulary. I have sticky notes all over my classroom too, so I can learn French while I'm at work. Everything is labeled—*le papier, le piano, la table.* Once I walked in after recess and Michael had put a sticky note on his forehead. It said *"le boy."*

Grace believes in complete immersion. She speaks to me only in French. Usually I am completely lost and just stare at her. And I have become very good at nodding that I understand when really I don't.

In my lessons I am not allowed to even ask a question in English. If I try, Grace says, *"Non, non, en français. En français."*

Once in a while I beg her to explain a word in English, and she will. But that is rare. My lessons are one hour long. By the end of each lesson, my brain is so full, I cannot concentrate anymore.

Now I understand a little better what it is like to be Tomoya. Tomoya moved here from Japan at the beginning of the school year. When he entered my class, he spoke three words of English. He knew "yes," "no," and "toilet." Tomoya was a serious little boy. He didn't smile a lot.

For months Tomoya sat in the first row with a puzzled expression on his face—five days a week, six hours a day, trying understand his new American teacher who used too many hard words and spoke too fast. And unlike me, Tomoya could not ask the teacher to clarify something in Japanese when he did not understand.

I have a new appreciation for kids like Tomoya. In fact, I think one of the best things I ever did as a teacher was start learning French.

I know what it is like to sit at a desk while the teacher is waiting for the answer and I'm still trying to figure out the question.

I know how it feels when I say something and the teacher stares at me, trying to decipher what I just said.

I know how it feels to try so hard to remember the word I learned yesterday because I really do know it.

I know what it feels like to see the paper that I worked so hard on covered with corrections because I got all the plurals wrong.

I know how it feels to leave out all the articles and put everything in the present tense because it is easier.

And I know what it feels like when I'm tired and I just don't want to practice my foreign language today.

It always amazes me how fast kids pick up new languages. You should see Tomoya now. He reads. He writes. He talks in line.

Katie speaks German. Peter speaks Polish. Amanda speaks only Spanish at home, and so does Carlos. What a gift they all have to be able to speak, read, write, and think in more than one language. Not only are they developing a lifelong ability to communicate with more people, they are also developing a deeper understanding of their own and other cultures. And they are enhancing their ability in their mother tongues as well.

I wish someone had told me how important this was. I wish I had begun learning a language when I was young. I wish I had learned a foreign language in elementary school.

Last week Dawn got a new student. Her name is Haruna. Haruna is Japanese and speaks very little English, just like Tomoya when he first arrived. One day Haruna started to cry in class. Dawn tried to find out what was wrong but couldn't understand her. Haruna just cried.

Dawn sent me a note. "Please send Tomoya right away."

Tomoya went to Dawn's room and translated for Haruna. Her stomach ached. Tomoya went to the nurse's office and translated for the nurse. Tomoya went to the office and helped the sec-

retary when she called home to tell Haruna's mom. And Tomoya stayed with Haruna until her mother arrived at school.

At the end of the day Cathy came into my room.

"I'd like to speak with Tomoya, please," Cathy said.

Tomoya froze.

"Tomoya, Miss Carlson would like to speak with you," I said.

He looked straight ahead.

"Tomoya," said Miss Carlson, "I heard about what you did today and how you helped Haruna and everybody else, and I came to thank you."

Cathy looked at me.

"Mr. Done," she said, "if we ever need a translator, I know where to go."

Tomoya said nothing. He looked down and stared at his desk. Cathy looked at me as if maybe he did not understand her. But he understood perfectly. I could tell. The corners of his mouth went up. He was trying very hard not to smile.

"Thanks for your help, Katie," I said. "Are you having fun in the play?"

She stopped sweeping and smiled.

"Mr. Done," she said, "I can't wait for tomorrow. My whole family is coming—my dad and my mom and my brother and my grandma and my grandpa. And my dad is taking off work. You know, Mr. Done, this is my first play. Did you know that? And next year I want to be in another play. And when I grow up I want to be an actress. Did you know that, Mr. Done?"

I looked at her. Now I remembered why I do a musical with over ninety third graders every year. Now I remembered.

# Licorice

*I started out* the year with three hamsters, two guinea pigs, one rabbit, one parakeet, and a goldfish. Now, I'm down to two hamsters and one rabbit. I know what you're thinking. You're thinking that I don't take care of my animals. But that's not it. I *do* take care of them. I just lose them.

Humphrey was my favorite hamster. One day Ji Soo went to feed Humphrey, and he was gone. I have no idea how he got out of that cage. It was called the Alcatraz. But he escaped.

We searched everywhere for Humphrey. Kenny and Aaron made giant reward posters saying, "Have you seen this hamster?" Melanie drew Humphrey's face on each one, and Humphrey appeared on every telephone pole in town. But after about a week there was still no sign of him. Everyday the kids asked me, "When is Humphrey going to come back?"

"I think Humphrey went on a long, long trip," I finally said.

Lucy was our class parakeet. We loved Lucy. And Lucy loved to sing. Her favorite song was "One Hundred Bottles of Beer on the Wall." Brian taught it to her. It was a little embarrassing when she broke out into song in the middle of parent-teacher conferences. One day Michael took Lucy outside to clean her cage. He slid the bottom tray out, turned the cage upside down, and we all waved good-bye to Lucy.

I am a little embarrassed to tell you about Sam. Sam was a goldfish. How one loses a goldfish, I'll never know. But one day he was there, and the next day he wasn't. I think it was my fault. The day before Sam disappeared, I read *The Cat in the Hat* to the class. Sam must have been listening too and tried to be like the fish in the book. Never read *The Cat in the Hat* in front of a goldfish.

Last week Stephen came up to me before school carrying a big bucket.

"Look, Mr. Done!" he said, lifting the lid.

I jumped back.

"Can we keep him?" Stephen begged.

Inside the bucket was a twelve-foot black boa constrictor. OK, so it wasn't twelve feet. But it was a snake, and I hate snakes.

"Who put him in the bucket?" I asked.

"My mom," said Stephen.

"Does your mom know you brought him here?"

"She told me to."

I grinned. "Tell your mom 'thanks.' "

Would someone please tell all the mommies to stop sending me their hamsters and mice and guinea pigs and bunnies and boa constrictors that they don't want anymore? This is not a petting zoo. I am not running a pet store. And I am *not* Old MacDonald.

"Please can we keep it?" Stephen begged some more.

I sighed. Then I heard the little teacher voice inside my head.

It said, "Animals are good for children. Animals teach them re-sponsibility. Animals bring warmth to a classroom. Look how ex-cited the boy is."

Sometimes I *hate* that little voice.

"OK," I said, "but I'm not getting near that thing. What's his name? Killer?"

"Licorice," said Stephen.

We put Killer into a glass terrarium. I cut a wire screen for the top and laid three bricks on it.

A couple of days later, Stephen went to feed the snake.

"Mr. Done, Licorice isn't there," Stephen said.

"Stephen, stop foolin' around."

"No, *really,* Mr. Done. He's not there," Stephen said again.

Everyone looked at the cage.

"Stephen, that's not funny," I said.

"Mr. Done, *really!*" he shouted.

Everyone stared at me.

I froze. Certainly he was kidding. I got up, walked over to the cage, and looked inside. Killer was gone.

I screamed. Instantly fifteen kids ran over to the cage. The rest jumped onto their chairs and desks. Emily ran out of the room.

I shouted, "OK, everyone. Sit down. Sit down."

For the next thirty minutes we searched the desks and the cupboards and the closets and the file cabinets. But no Killer. At morning recess I told Cathy what happened. She sent in the cus-todian. He searched the room too. Still no luck.

I tried to teach that day. But all they wanted to do was look for the snake and ask, "Mr. Done, where do you think Licorice is?" again and again.

Cathy came in as we were looking inside the piano.

"Any luck?" she asked.

"No. We've looked everywhere. I can't teach in here knowing Killer's loose," I said.

She laughed.

"All they want to do is try to scare me," I said. "Brian opened his backpack this morning and screamed, 'Snake!' Ryan reached into his desk during reading and yelled, 'I'm bit!' Patrick put his hand in the ball box and pretended he was attacked. I can't handle it!"

She laughed some more.

"It's not funny!" I shouted. Then I looked at the door.

"But maybe he slid under the door," I said, pointing to the one-inch gap between the door and the floor. "See that crack? He probably slid right under it. Guess he could be anywhere in the building, don't you think?"

Cathy ran out of the room.

Soon we all forgot about Killer. We pretty much figured that he had found his way outside somehow.

A couple of days later we were all gathered together in the multipurpose room for our weekly assembly. Cathy stood in the front of the room. The teachers sat on blue metal folding chairs with the name of the school stenciled in black letters on the back of each one (I think they stenciled them the year Dylan made off with the projector cart). Mrs. Turner and Mrs. Stewart, who had been sorting through the costumes from the play, stopped by to see the children. The kids sat in rows on the floor, the kindergarteners in the front, the fifth graders in the back.

School assembly time is the time when children like to demonstrate how many different ways they can sit on the floor. My students are quite skilled at it. Anthony can stretch his legs out all the way (even with a second grader seated five inches in front of him). Brian can sit really high on his knees and block the vision of an entire fourth grade class. And Justin can lie down when the room is packed and show you how to make snow angels on the tiles.

After twenty minutes of saying, "Sit up," and "Sit down," and "Move up," and "Move over," I finally moved Anthony and Brian and Justin right by me. Anthony sat on my right, Brian on my left, and Justin sat between my legs. (You can always tell a lot about kids by how close they are sitting to the teacher at the morning assembly.)

So there we were. Mrs. Fisher had just finished leading us in our school song, and Cathy walked up to the microphone to pass out the Citizen of the Month certificates and this month's happy birthday pencils.

"Boys and girls," Cathy began, "now we will—"

All of a sudden there was a scream from the back of the room. We all whipped around. Just as we turned around, a large shopping bag went flying through the air and landed in the middle of the second graders. Out flew a dozen Indian tunics and one black snake. Mrs. Turner was standing on a folding chair shaking and pointing at the center of the room.

In a flash everyone was on their feet. The second graders ran for the sides. The third graders ran for the center. The fourth graders followed the third graders. Some of the first graders started crying. Everyone was talking at once and trying to get a look at Killer.

*"Get the snake!"* I screamed at Stephen.

Cathy shouted into the microphone for everyone to sit down.

Stephen caught Killer.

Cathy shouted into the microphone again, but everyone kept talking. Finally she gave up and adjourned the assembly.

With Killer safe in Stephen's hands, I got off my chair and started walking my kids back to the classroom. Mrs. Turner was now seated and fanning herself; she was surrounded by other room moms. I stopped and asked her what had happened. She said that she was holding the bag of costumes when she felt something on her arm. She thought it was her youngest daughter grabbing her hand and didn't think anything of it, but when she looked down, she saw a snake sliding out of the bag and up her arm. So she threw the bag.

When we got back to the room, everyone wanted to tell the story over and over again because of course everyone saw exactly what had happened. Carlos stood on his chair and pretended to be Mrs. Turner. Anthony pretended that he was Killer and dove across the room. I put Killer in an old aquarium (Houdini couldn't have gotten his way out of that thing!) and made Stephen stand guard till school was over. After the last bell, I sent Stephen home with Killer and a note for his mom.

Dear Mrs. Moore,

    It was so nice of you to send your snake to school with Stephen. The children learned so much about snakes. We learned how to hunt for reptiles in a piano. We learned how to get ready to jump backward before opening the paint cupboard. We learned that the crack under the door is exactly 2.5 centimeters. We learned that snakes must like the smell of coffee and can fly thirty feet across a crowded room. Thank you for helping us learn so much about snakes.

Yours sincerely,
Mr. Done

# Gifted

*There once was* a student named Phillip. Phillip's fourth grade teacher, Mr. Donaldson, recommended that Phillip be tested for the gifted program. At that time the program was called MGM; the initials stood for Mentally Gifted Minors.

One day Phillip went to the office to see a lady he had never seen before. She spoke in a strong southern accent and wore lots of perfume. Phillip knew why he was there. She was going to give him a test to see if he was gifted.

Of course Phillip already knew that he was gifted. His mom had always told him he was. His teachers had told him too. The lady asked Phillip a lot of questions and Phillip answered them.

Two weeks later Phillip's mom received a letter from the school. It said that Phillip could not be in the gifted program. He cried.

The next year Phillip's fifth grade teacher, Mrs. Sezaki, recommended that Phillip be tested for the gifted program again. So Phillip went to see the testing lady a second time. She still had a strong accent and wore lots of perfume. Again she asked a lot of questions and Phillip answered them.

Two weeks later Phillip's mom received a letter from the school. It said that Phillip was gifted now. He did not understand how he could not be gifted one year and then be gifted the next. It must be, he thought, because he learned his times tables faster.

So Phillip left his fifth grade class twice a week after lunch with a few other students and went to the gifted class. Once they rode in a bus to the theater and saw a play by George Bernard Shaw. Once they visited the space museum. Once they made wrapping paper. Phillip did not understand why his friends could not go with him to the play or the space museum, or make wrapping paper. He knew that they would also like to meet the astronaut.

Phillip did not want to be gifted anymore. Back in his classroom, his friends were making dioramas out of shoe boxes. He wanted to make a diorama too. He asked his mom if he could stop going to the gifted class and make a diorama. She said yes.

Why do we have gifted education? Why is there such a strong lobby for gifted education? I will tell you why. It feeds egos. People can say, "My child is in the gifted program." Now, please don't get me wrong. I'm all for challenging students. I'm all for meeting the individual needs of children. I'm all for enrichment—as long as every child is being enriched.

Let me tell you how some of these gifted programs work. In some districts children who are "identified" as gifted get pulled out of their regular classrooms once, maybe twice a month for "enrichment." The students usually work on projects that are supposed to be more challenging, more enriching, more "higher-level." Well, I've seen what they bring back.

"Uh . . . that's a very nice plant holder. You macraméed it in the gifted class?"

"Oh, you made a bird house in your gifted class today? It's lovely. I didn't realize that hammering was so higher-level."

Sometimes the gifted students go on field trips. They might visit a gallery or attend a concert or go on a boat trip.

And what about those students who are left behind? I'd like you to see their faces when the "gifted" ones leave. The ones left behind are sad. They feel dumb. They do not understand. Teachers spend the whole year building their kids up and telling them how special and smart and talented and wonderful they are, and then it's ruined.

What do I say to the ones left behind? Sorry, Johnny, you can jump higher and run faster than any student in the school, but you struggle in reading, so you're not gifted. Sorry, Becky, you can play Mozart and Beethoven and Chopin beautifully, but you cannot read big numbers, so you're not gifted. Sorry, Alexis, you can draw ten times better than I can and you're only eight years old, but you missed one too many problems on the test, so you're not gifted. And sorry, Stephen, you can whip anyone in chess and put together the most elaborate Lego invention, but you can't spell, so you're not gifted.

I am not a political person. I never have been. I am too busy teaching children the difference between *there* and *their* and *they're*. But this issue riles me up. You can overload my classroom.

You can go three years without giving me a raise. You can ration my paper to two reams a month. You can make me teach my own art and PE and music because of budget cuts. You can take away the school nurse and the counselor and the librarian and my hot lunch. You can make me buy my own pencils and stickers and rewards and soccer balls. But don't start messing with my students.

# Open House

*Every spring* at my school we have Open House. It's the night when all the moms and dads come to school to see their kids' work. And the kids come too.

At our school, Open House is a big deal—even bigger than Back to School Night. Teachers spend weeks getting ready. The Model Homes lay out extra plastic runners. The Pilers straighten their piles. The Shocks decorate the pencil sharpeners. And the Hospitals dare to poke holes in their bulletin boards. Kim's name for Open House is Cecil B. DeMille Presents. Lisa calls it the Super Bowl. I call it Barnum and Bailey.

When the parents arrive, they come with their shopping lists in hand. You see, the parents are supposed to visit their own child's classroom and look at their child's work. But I usually have just as many parents of second graders as parents of third graders. They are shopping for next year's teacher.

This year for Barnum and Bailey all the third grade classes made huge murals of the water cycle. I was just putting the finishing touches on mine when I ran out of cottonballs.

Crap, I thought. I have to finish this mural. You can't have a water cycle mural without clouds. I went to Mrs. Wilson's room, but her door was locked. I didn't have time to run to the store. So I ran to the nurse's office. Nurses always have cottonballs.

I looked in all the cupboards. No luck. Then suddenly I spotted a box under the sink. I snatched the box, hid it under my jacket, and ran back to my classroom. When I got back, I started attaching my new clouds. Perfect!

Just as I was finishing up the last few clouds, Dawn walked into my room.

"All ready?" she asked.

"Just about," I replied.

"It looks great."

"Thanks."

Dawn stared at the mural. Her eyes got big.

"Don't tell me," she said slowly.

"What?" I asked.

"Those are *not* what I think they are," she said.

"What?" I asked again.

"The clouds."

"You like 'em?" I asked proudly.

She closed her eyes. "You're *not* using minipads for clouds, are you?"

"You can tell?"

"Uh . . . yes," she said. "Where did you get them?"

I smiled. "In the nurse's office."

She shook her head and started walking out the door. "Well," she said under her breath, "at least you didn't find tampons."

# Grammar Lessons

*Today, boys and girls,* we are going to study the parts of speech. We will start with the word *boy. Boy* is a noun. A noun is a person, place, or thing. The word *teacher* is also a noun. Can you all say "noun"?

Now, there are two types of nouns—common nouns and proper nouns. *Boy* is a common noun. *Stephen* is a proper noun. Proper nouns are more specific than common nouns. Proper nouns are always capitalized. *Teacher* is a common noun. *Mr. Done* is a proper noun. Understand?

Adjectives describe nouns. *Naughty* is an adjective. It describes the boy. *Angry* is also an adjective; it describes the teacher.

In the sentence, "Mr. Done chases Stephen," *chases* is a verb. Verbs show action. When "Mr. Done catches Stephen," *catches* is the verb.

A pronoun takes the place of a noun. In the sentence, "He takes Stephen to the principal's office," *he* replaces *Mr. Done.* Thus, *he* is a pronoun. If we say, for example, "Mr. Done takes him to the principal's office," *him* is the pronoun.

Prepositional phrases modify verbs. "To the principal's office" is what we call a prepositional phrase, for it modifies the verb *takes.* In the sentence, "Mr. Done and Stephen walk down the hall," *down the hall* is a prepositional phrase. If I say, "The angry teacher waits for the principal," can you find the prepositional phrase?

"Mr. Done talks with the principal" is a simple sentence. A simple sentence contains only one subject and one predicate. In this sentence, *Mr. Done* is the subject, and *talks with the principal* is the predicate. "Mr. Done is not very happy right now" and "Stephen is in big trouble" are also simple sentences. Each has only one subject and one predicate.

A compound sentence is a sentence that contains two or more independent clauses. "The principal listened to Mr. Done, and he immediately called Stephen's parents" contains two independent clauses: "The principal listened to Mr. Done" and "he immediately called Stephen's parents." As you can see, the clauses are connected by the word *and*. *And* is what we call a coordinating conjunction; it connects the two independent clauses.

Subordinate clauses cannot stand alone. Let's look at the following sentence: "Mom, who has been called out of an important meeting at work, drives to school to pick up Stephen." In this example, "who has been called out of an important meeting" cannot stand by itself. "Stephen, who is sitting in the principal's office, is very nervous" also contains a subordinate clause. Can you identify it?

When Mom arrives at school and asks, "What happened?" she is asking a question. Note that a question ends with a question mark. If Mom says, "I'm not happy about this," this is not a question. This is a declarative statement. Declarative statements do not end with question marks.

In the previous example, you can see that *I* and *am* have been connected with an apostrophe to form the word *I'm*. This is what we call a contraction. "You're in big trouble, sonny!" also contains a contraction. "I don't know what I'm going to do with you!" contains two contractions.

At this point Mom is most likely using a lot of exclamatory sentences. Exclamatory sentences end with exclamation marks. Exclamatory sentences express surprise or emotion or deep feeling. Right now, Mom is probably expressing all three. "You're grounded for a month!" is an exclamatory sentence. "Wait till we get home!" is also an exclamatory sentence. (Note that the first sentence also contains a contraction.)

The exclamation mark is also used after commands (statements that require immediate action). "Get in the car!" is a command. Here Mom is commanding Stephen to do something. Sometimes a sentence will have more than one exclamation mark. When Mom screams, "Oh! Just wait till your father hears about this!" we can see two exclamation marks, one following the word *Oh* (this is called an interjection), and one at the end of the sentence.

When Mom screams, "Stephen Eric, you're grounded for a month, you lose your allowance, and you have no TV for the rest of your life!" these three exclamations are separated by commas. A colon may be used here as well. Mom could say, "Stephen Eric, listen very closely to the following: you're grounded for a month, you lose your allowance, and you have no TV for the rest of your life!"

Idioms are expressions that cannot be directly translated. Every language has them. If Mom says, "Stephen, you're in the doghouse!" this does not mean that Mom will put Stephen in a doghouse. It means that Stephen is in trouble. If Stephen says, "Mom hit the roof," he means that Mom is extremely angry.

When we use the words *like, as,* or *than* to compare two things, we're using similes. "Mom blew up like a volcano," "Mom is as mad as a hornet," and "Mom is madder than a wet hen!" are all examples of similes—and are all probably true.

Metaphors are different from similes. Metaphors compare two things but do not use the words *like* or *as* or *than.* "Mom was a volcano!" is a metaphor. We know that Mom is not really a volcano. We are saying this descriptively. "Stephen is dead meat" is also a metaphor. He is not really dead meat (well, not yet anyway). We mean that he is in big trouble.

When Stephen responds, "I didn't do anything!" this is neither a metaphor nor a simile. This is what we call a lie.

# School Supplies

*It's embarrassing.* No matter how hard I try, every year my kids still confuse the basic items in the classroom. It's April, and Joshua still thinks his desk is a wastebasket. Joey thinks the ball is a chair, and Patrick thinks his pencil is a Q-tip! I had to do something. I could not send my kids out into the world like this.

I could just see it. Someday Joshua will take his desk out to the curb on garbage pickup day. Joey will furnish his dining room with Hoppity Hops, and Patrick will go deaf. And it will be all my fault. Something had to be done. So I decided to make a huge sign and post it in the front of my classroom. Here's what it says:

## Attention All Students!

1. These are scissors. We cut paper with them. We do not cut our hair with them. We do not cut our friend's hair with them either.
2. This is a pen cap. It goes on top of the marker. Then you can use your marker more than once and not ask me tomorrow why we have no more black markers.
3. This is masking tape. We do not play kidnap with it and tape

Ryan's mouth shut to see if you can understand what Ryan is saying when his mouth is covered with tape.

4. This is a permanent pen. See the word *permanent* on the side. We use it to write on paper. We do not use it to write our friend's phone number on the palm of our hand. We do not use it to draw tattoos on our arms either.

5. These are my car keys. We do not play hide-and-seek with them.

6. This is my coffee mug. (See #5.)

7. This is a paper clip. It holds papers together. It is not a retainer. You do not have braces.

8. This is a coat hook. It holds things. The coat hook and the jacket are friends. They like to be together.

9. This is a yardstick. We measure with it. It is not a sword. It is not a hockey stick. It is not a golf club. It is not a javelin. It is not a spear.

10. This is Kleenex. We blow our nose with it.

11. This is an empty wastebasket. This is what you put the Kleenex in after you have just blown your nose.

12. This is a desk. It is not the wastebasket. It is not a toy box either. It is not the Hello Kitty store.

13. This is a doormat. You wipe your feet on it after you have run around outside in the mud and the snow.

14. This is a carpet. See the footprints. This is how a carpet looks after you do not use the doormat.

15. This is a drinking fountain. We drink water from it. It is not a birdbath. It is not a shower. It is not a Super Soaker.

16. This is a newspaper. We put the newspaper under our painting before we decide to paint on the carpet.

17. This is carpet cleaner. This is what we use to clean the carpet that you just painted on.

18. This is your lunch bag. It is not a bomb. We do not blow it up and see how loud it will explode.

19. This is a juice box. It is not a bomb either.

20. This is a paintbrush. We dip it in paint and paint the paper.

21. This is a student. We do not paint the student.

22. This is a telephone. It makes phone calls. Watch me push these buttons on the telephone to call your mom because you just painted Erika.

23. This is a chair. We do not stand on it. We do not hurdle it. We do not walk on it. We sit on it.

24. This is a seatbelt. It will be attached to your chair soon if you do not put your bottom on that seat right this second!

# How Old Is Your Mom?

*I don't know why,* but kids like to talk about their parents' ages. It is as predictable a subject of conversation as what they're going to be for Halloween or whether or not Santa Claus really exists. Every year, at some time, I will hear one student ask another, "How old is your mom?"

I remember when I first heard the question. I was twenty-three years old and fresh out of college.

"How old is your mom?" Kelly asked Tiffany.

"She's thirty-five," answered Tiffany.

"My mom's thirty-seven," said Kelly.

Wow, I thought to myself. Their parents are old!

Pretty soon I was thirty-three, and I heard the question again.

"How old is your dad?" Benjamin asked Alex.

"He's thirty-five," answered Alex.

"My dad's thirty-four," said Benjamin.

"My dad's thirty-three," said Danny.

Wow, I thought. I'm the same age as their parents now.

Now I am forty-three. And sure enough, this year I heard the question again.

"How old is your mom?" Melanie asked Isabel while they were coloring their Mother's Day cards.

"My mom's thirty-five," Isabel said.

"How old is your dad?" Melanie asked.

"He's old," Isabel answered. "He's thirty-six."

Oh my God, I thought. I'm older than their parents. What happened?

Last summer I ran into Mrs. White in the grocery store parking lot. I had had her daughter in third grade.

"How's Stephanie doing?" I asked Mrs. White.

"Oh, she's doing just great. She's tearing 'em up at Stanford."

"Stanford?" I screamed.

"Yes, she's a junior."

"A junior! She can't be. She was just eight years old. She can't be in college yet. She just learned how to multiply! She just learned her cursive!"

The other day I went to the bank and walked up to the counter.

"Hi, Mr. Done," said the bank teller.

"Uh . . . hi," I said.

Behind the counter stood a beautiful woman.

"Remember me?" she asked. "Julia Velazquez?"

I jogged my memory banks.

A pudgy little eight-year-old girl with headgear popped into my head. I remember she could not add.

"Yes." I nodded. "Yes, I remember you. You're . . . all grown up."

She smiled.

"How old are you now, Julia?" I asked.

"Twenty-four," she answered.

I stared at her.

"Twenty-four?" I said, shocked.

Julia laughed.

"This is my son," she said, pointing to a photo next to her computer of a cute little kid. "He just turned two."

I was speechless.

Julia gave me my money (I checked her addition). I thanked her, then said good-bye. I walked out of the bank, opened my car door, and sat in my car. I did not start the engine.

I thought to myself, Where did the time go?

Teachers are Peter Pans in a way. It's so easy to lose track of time. You forget that you're getting older, because they're always eight years old. You teach in the same classroom year after year. You wear the same tie. You tell the same jokes. Everything is always the same.

Then one day you are kicked into the reality that you are getting older when you receive a graduation announcement or a wedding invitation, or when the bank teller says, "Hi, Mr. Done. Remember me?"

Twenty-four years old! I said to myself. I'm getting old.

Then I made a decision. Right there in the car. I decided that the day one of my students says to me, "Mr. Done, you taught my mom when she was in third grade," *that* is the day I will retire.

# Words You Cannot Say in Class

*It is well known* among teachers that there are certain words you must never say in the classroom. Take the seventh planet from the sun, for example. I would like to talk with the person who came up with the name Uranus. Obviously he never taught third graders. Saturn is a perfectly lovely name for a planet. And so is Jupiter. But Uranus? *What* was he thinking? I've tried accenting the wrong syllables in that word. I've tried mispronouncing it completely. It makes no difference. No matter how you pronounce it, Uranus always sounds bad. One year I finally got smart and said there are no planets after Jupiter.

I don't teach about Columbus anymore either. Well, OK, I do, but I stay clear of those ships. Especially the diagrams. Inevitably, when you pass out diagrams of the *Niña* and the *Pinta* and the *Santa Maria,* the first thing they find is the poop deck. Who the hell named it the poop deck!

Studying geography can be dangerous too. One day we were all reading about the Galápagos Islands in our science books, and we turned to the page on bird life. I started reading aloud. Do you know what happens to third graders when you say "blue-footed booby"? They do not continue to read. They do not hear you say, "Stop!" and "Enough!" and "Get off the ceiling!" because they are too busy laughing and shouting, "Blue-footed booby!" six hundred times.

Even in art, one has to be careful. Once we were making construction paper flags for President's Day.

"OK, boys and girls," I said, "Everyone take your strips and—"

Justin began to snicker.

"Justin, what is so funny?" I asked.

"Nothing," he answered.

I continued. "OK, now, everyone take your red strips and glue them onto the—"

Justin started laughing again.

I stared at him. "Justin, *what* is so funny?"

"You said 'strip,' " he said, trying not to burst out laughing.

"Yes. So what," I said.

"Like strip naked!" he exploded. Then he fell out of his seat and started rolling on the floor.

I stared at him in disbelief.

The last time I had seen him act like this was when Mrs. Turner asked him if he wanted a weenie at the Back to School Barbecue. (By the way, would someone please tell the room moms that they are *hot dogs?*)

As you know, sometimes kids will mispronounce words. One day James said "fighted." So I corrected him.

"James, the word is 'fought,' " I said.

He started giggling.

"What's so funny?" I asked.

"You said 'fart,' " said James.

"I did not!" I said firmly. "I said 'fought'!" Then I said it again very slowly.

"See!" James screamed. "You said 'fart'!" and he started laughing again.

Have you ever tried to say "fought" slowly? Go ahead, try it. Stop reading this and try it.

See? James was right. When you say "fought" slowly, it sounds like you're saying "fart" with a British accent.

But arguing with James was nothing compared to last week's Spring Concert. At the end of the performance I stood up in front of two hundred kindergarten, first, second, and third graders, and all their parents and said, "I'd like to thank our wonderful pianist, Mrs. Fisher!"

The parents applauded. The children began to laugh. I gave them the Chin Up. I knew exactly what they were thinking. So I looked straight at them all and repeated myself very slowly.

*"Pi-an-ist!"* I said.

Well, no child *ever* hears the final *t* in that word. No child *wants* to hear the final *t* in that word. It is much more fun to *not* hear the *t* in that word. Justin, of course, had to be carried out on a stretcher.

One even has to be careful giving spelling tests. One day I handed out the week's spelling list and began reviewing the words. "OK, boys and girls," I said, "our first spelling word is 'happy.' Can you all say 'happy'?"

"Happy," everyone chanted.

"Good," I said. " 'Happy' is spelled 'h-a-p-p-y.' Let's spell it out together."

Everyone spelled out loud, "H-a-p-p . . ."

"Look!" Michael shouted. There's 'p-p' in that word!"

Everyone laughed.

"Yes, Michael, there are two *p*s in that word. Now settle down."

I continued.

"OK, everyone, let's look at the next word, shall we? Can you read the next word for us please, Emily?" I asked.

"Dis-ap-pear," she read.

"Good, Emily," I said.

Michael shouted, "There's peepee in that word too!"

"Michael, I know someone who is going to disappear very soon if he doesn't get ahold of himself right now!" I said firmly.

Then I glanced down at the next few words: "wrapping," "stepping," "shopping."

I sighed. Great, I thought. It's the peepee list.

Who was the wise guy who thought of doubling that stupid *p* to make the vowel short? Obviously he never knew Michael. Obviously he never taught elementary school. Why, I'll bet he was the same bozo who named all the planets, and the parts of a ship, and the birds on the Galápagos Islands!

# Countdown

# Miss Greco

*When I was in second grade,* my teacher's name was Miss Greco. She was old. She wore big gold earrings and smelled like my grandma. In December she wore a Christmas tree pin. Sometimes I would wear my older brother's hand-me-down suits and ties to school, and Dippity-do my hair just so she'd say I looked nice. She always did.

Miss Greco taught me how to clap big words into syllables, how to add big numbers, and how to spell *environment*. But, she taught me something else too—something no other teacher ever did.

You see, everyday after lunch we had silent reading. While we read, Miss Greco usually worked on some sort of project at her desk in front of the classroom. During this time, I watched closely as she turned newspapers into puppets, baby food jars into Christmas presents, and egg cartons into bumble bees. Miss Greco could turn an old sheet into a kimono, a road map into wrapping paper, and a basket into a Munchkin hat. She was magic.

Miss Greco showed me how to make something out of nothing. She showed me what thinking looked like. She showed me how to create. Of course I didn't know it at the time, but Miss Greco was showing me how to be a teacher.

Today I still wear gel in my hair. I still wear a tie to school. I still have silent reading after lunch. And sometimes I too will use silent reading time to design or make something. And almost always when I glance up from whatever it is I'm making, one or two sets of eyes will be on me.

I do not tell them to get back to their reading. For surely they have lost their places by now. Maybe they are learning how to be teachers too. If so, I hope they will be like Miss Greco.

# Tell Us a Story!

*Miss Greco* was a great storyteller. I remember when we were all wilting, or wound up, or worn out, she'd ring her silver bell, let us put our heads down on our desks, then begin to tell us a story. We were riveted.

I loved Miss Greco's stories, and I still remember them. Once during the war, she sold peanut brittle door to door. Once she drove an ice cream truck. Once when she was young, she took an umbrella into the shower and pretended it was raining. Once she met John F. Kennedy. And once she had a German shepherd that would do the shopping for her. It's true.

Her dog's name was Mitzi. Miss Greco would put her shopping list and an envelope with money into a basket, and Mitzi would walk down the street to the butcher with the basket in her mouth. When Mitzi arrived at the butchershop, she'd put down the basket and scratch the door till the butcher came outside. The butcher would take out the list and the money, put the items and change into the basket, and give Mitzi a hot dog, and Mitzi would walk back home with the groceries.

I tell my students stories too. I don't know what it is, but when a teacher starts telling children anything about his own

242 • Phillip Done

life—anything at all—they will remember every word he says, then go home and tell everything to their mothers.

## For When They're Driving Me Crazy

"Did I tell you The Raisin Bread Story? I can't believe I didn't tell you The Raisin Bread Story! Well, when I was a baby, I would not sit still—not for a minute. My mom would try to hold me and I would crawl all over her. Once she was in the kitchen ready to throw me out the window when she spotted a loaf of raisin bread on the counter. She threw the loaf of raisin bread onto the linoleum, plopped me down next to it, and said, 'Pick out *all* the raisins!' I picked out the raisins, and my mom had five minutes of peace.

"Now here, do this worksheet!"

## For When They Are Tardy

"Did I tell you The Thermometer Story? I thought everyone knew that. Once when I was a kid, I didn't want to go to school. So I pretended I couldn't get up. My mom came in and told me to get up. I moaned and said I was sick. She got the thermometer, shook it, and put it in my mouth and left the room. While she was gone, I got up, lit a match (which I had hidden), and put it under the thermometer. After a few minutes I jumped back into bed and put the thermometer back under my tongue. Soon my mom came back into my bedroom and took the thermometer out of my mouth. She looked at it, then looked at me, then looked back at the thermometer. 'You know what it says?' she asked. 'You have a temperature of a hundred and ten. You should be dead. Now rise, Lazarus, and go to school.'

"So, why are you late?"

## For When They Forget Something

"Did I tell you The Show Story? I didn't? It's famous. Well, when I was in high school, I was in a musical called *Gypsy*. In one part we had a superfast costume change, and I had twenty-five seconds to change from a military costume to pajamas. Well, in order to make the costume change and be back onstage in time for the next scene, I had to put the pajamas on underneath the military costume. It was faster this way.

"I remember it was closing night. The house was full. The lights went black. I ran off stage left, whipped off my uniform, and screamed! You know why? I had forgotten to put my pajama bottoms on. So yours truly did the whole next scene in his pajama shirt and boxers.

"Now, you can bring your homework tomorrow."

## For When They Are Boarding the Bus

"Did I tell you The Camping Story? No? You're kidding. Once my family went camping with my uncle and his family. We drove in two station wagons. My uncle had four kids and we had four kids. All the cousins mixed up in the two cars—some in one, some in the other. Well, we stopped at the supermarket on the way to the campgrounds and went shopping for the trip. After we finished shopping, we drove to the campgrounds. At the campgrounds, my dad asked my uncle where I was. My uncle thought I was in my dad's car. My dad thought I was in my uncle's car. Then they both realized that they had left me back at the supermarket. Immediately my parents jumped into my dad's car and raced back to the store. I was sitting out in front of the store in one of those little firetrucks that shake when you put in a quarter. My mom was crying and crying. 'Hi, Mom,' I said. 'Do you have a quarter?' I didn't even know they were gone.

"Now, stay with your group today. And don't go wondering off, OK?"

## For When They Embarrass Themselves

"You don't know The Spaghetti Story? It's a classic! Well, when I was in college learning how to become a teacher, I worked at a spaghetti restaurant. It was my first day on my own. I remember I made ten salads, put them on a big tray, lifted the tray onto my shoulder, and walked out of the kitchen into the restaurant. As I was walking to the table, I did not see the scoop of butter on the floor. I slipped on the butter and screamed, trying to hold onto the tray. Everyone froze. I teetered around the room, trying not to lose my grip. But finally, down the tray went. Blue cheese and thousand island and creamy Italian flew everywhere. Then the whole restaurant applauded. I had to clean it all up, then go back and make ten more salads.

"Now, I'll clean this up. Go back and get another lunch."

## For When Teacher Doesn't Want to Teach Anything in Last Ten Minutes on Friday

"Did I tell you The Spider-Man Story? I didn't? Well, put down your pencils. That's my best story of all. You see, when I was in high school, my dad lent me the car. It was a Chrysler New Yorker. One night I was leaving my friend's house when I looked across the street and saw two men in the Chrysler. They were starting the engine. Oh my God, I thought. They're hot-wiring my dad's car! I ran across the street as fast as I could, screamed, *'Stop!'* and dove onto the car. Splat! I landed on the windshield just like Spider-Man. The two men froze. I saved the car. But as I lay there on the glass, I realized something.

"It wasn't my car.

"*My* car was parked right in front of them. It looked just like their car. Quickly I smiled, slithered off, opened my car door, and drove away.

"Well, it's time to go now. Have a good weekend. And don't go jumping on any windshields."

# How Many Times Have I Said That?

*As you know, I* have been studying French all year. And I am proud to say that I am now fluent. Really. I am completely fluent. Well, OK, I am fluent in French at school.

I came about it quite by accident, actually. You see, one day I got so tired of saying the same old things that teachers say over and over again that I decided to just start saying them in French. And *voilà!* The new lunch supervisor thought I was born in France. Cathy thinks I'm bilingual.

Believe me. It works. All you have to do is learn the French for the top ten phrases that teachers say, and you too can be fluent. Here they are:

| English | French |
|---|---|
| Walk! | *Ne cours pas!* |
| Sit down! | *Assieds-toi!* |
| Sh! | *Chut!* |
| Put that away! | *Range-ça immediatement!* |
| Quiet down! | *Silence!* |
| Put your name on your paper. | *Ecris ton nom sur ta feuille.* |
| You're excused. | *Tu peux y aller.* |

| | |
|---|---|
| How do you end a sentence? | *Comment est-ce-qu'on fini une phrase?* |
| Line up! | *Alignez-vous!* |
| Do I need to call your mom? | *Est-ce-que je dois appeller ta mère?* |

When you know these ten phrases, you do not just have to use them in the classroom. Oh no. I toss them around all over the place. If the clerk in Safeway asks me if I want paper or plastic, I speak French. It makes no sense, but they seem impressed. When I pick up my shirts at the drycleaners, I speak French too.

Only once did I have a problem. I was in the city library and the librarian said I owed $37.50 in overdue fines. I leaned over the counter, smiled at the librarian, and said, *"Est-ce-que je dois appeller ta mère?"* in my best French accent.

She leaned over to me and said, "No, but do I need to call yours?"

I paid the fine.

# Why Do I Teach?

*Every year* I ask my students what they want to be when they grow up. I tell their parents to listen closely. Because it was in third grade that I decided I wanted to become a teacher.

"When I grow up, I want to be a lawyer," said Amanda.

"I want to be a spy," said Justin.

"The doctor that helps animals," said Melanie.

"An actor," said Stephen.

"A doctor," said Anthony.

"Something that makes a lot of money," said Nicole.

"A baseball player," said Matthew.

"Does anyone want to be a teacher?" I asked.

"No way!" shouted Kevin.

"Why not?" I asked.

"I don't want to wear a tie," said Justin.

"My dad says teachers don't make any money," Aaron said.

"Well, that's true," I said. "Aaron, what does your dad do for work?"

"He's the vice president of some company," Aaron answered.

"Is he hiring?" I asked.

"Huh?"

"Never mind," I said.

Natalie raised her hand.

"Yes, Natalie?"

"Mr. Done, why did you become a teacher?" she asked.

"I like unclogging the drinking fountain." I smiled.

"No, come on, really," said Natalie. "Why did you become a teacher?"

It was a good question—one I hadn't thought about since my student teaching days. I thought about it for the rest of the day.

I became a teacher because I like that I get to start all over again every September.

I became a teacher because I like watching thirty-two silent, wide-eyed children suddenly burst into laughter all at the same time when the Grinch rides his sleigh down to Who-ville.

I like when one child starts singing and the others join in.

I like hearing them giggle to themselves when they're reading a new book during silent reading time.

I like to hand out those little candy hearts with the words on them around Valentine's Day and watch the kids scream if the hearts say, "Hug Me."

And I get a kick out of seeing kids carry trombone cases to school that are bigger than they are.

Why do I teach? Where else can you leave work and have hundreds of little people scream good-bye to you from the school bus every day?

But the main reason I became a teacher is that I like being the first one to introduce kids to words and music and books and people and numbers and concepts and ideas that they have never heard about or thought about before.

I like being the first one to tell them about Long John Silver and negative numbers and Beethoven and alliteration and "Oh, What a Beautiful Morning" and similes and right angles and Ebenezer Scrooge.

Can you remember exactly when you learned something new? I can. I remember where I was sitting when Miss Greco taught us "I'm Looking Over a Four-Leaf Clover." I remember when Mrs. Sezaki taught us what "discrimination" meant as she described her experiences in a Japanese internment camp in California. She called it a concentration camp. I remember exactly when Mr. Johnson taught me nine times seven with his magic multiplying marshmallows. I remember when Mrs. Garson told me there is no such word as "funner" and I didn't believe her.

Just think about what you know today. You read. You write. You work with numbers. You solve problems. We take all these things for granted. But of course you haven't always read. You haven't always known how to write. You weren't born knowing how to subtract 199 from 600. Someone showed you. There was a moment when you moved from not knowing to knowing. There was a moment when you moved from not understanding to understanding.

*That's* why I became a teacher.

# Out to Dinner with Teachers

*Last night* Dawn, Mike, Lisa, Kim, and I went out to dinner at a really nice restaurant to celebrate the last month of school. As you know, whenever we get together, we usually end up talking about school. So last night we all agreed—absolutely no school talk. Instead we talked about what normal people talk about.

We talked about art.
　　*"You should stop by and see Brian's new fresco on his desk."*

We talked about politics.
　　*"Melanie is circulating a petition to impeach the yard duty teacher."*

We talked about history.
　　*"Justin asked me today what a record player is."*

We talked about music.
　　*"Wait till Mrs. Fisher finds out that my entire class signed up to play the trumpet next year."*

We talked about fashion.

*"Did you get a load of what Cathy was wearing yesterday?"*

We talked about sports.

*"Who has the ball pump?"*

We talked about problems in society.

*"Three guesses who stopped up the urinals today."*

We talked about movies.

*"I just don't see Nicole Kidman as* Amelia Bedelia. *Do you?"*

We talked about food.

*"We'd like to start with five bowls of stone soup please."*

We talked about literature.

*"Boy, do I feel old. Charlie Brown is over fifty!"*

We talked about health care.

*"Have you seen the first-aid kit?"*

Then we all picked up our plates, walked to the dishwasher, threw the silverware into the silverware tub, and walked out of the restaurant.

# Customs

*Once a week* my kids go to science lab with Mrs. Simon. The kids love her. Mrs. Simon wears bug T-shirts and planet earrings. And she has a tarantula.

Mrs. Simon is always bringing in something fun to share with the children, like the static electricity machine that makes their hair stand up or a butterfly house or silkworms or my favorite—the potato-powered clock.

This spring we were studying the systems of the body, and Mrs. Simon brought in a real human skeleton. She borrowed it from a doctor friend but told the kids it was a third grader who didn't do his homework. The kids said it looked like me and named him Mr. Bone. So Mrs. Simon put a tie on him.

Seeing Mr. Bone reminded me of the time I tried to get my own collection of bones through customs.

Several years ago I took a leave of absence from my school district to teach at the American International School of Budapest. I had always wanted to teach overseas. And so I rented a storage unit, had a big garage sale, packed up, and flew to Hungary for a couple of years. It was a wonderful experience.

In the summers I would fly back home to visit my family and

friends, drink Campbell's soup, and order double caramel mac-
chiatos at Starbucks. When I flew back to Budapest, I always
brought an extra suitcase along full of Kraft macaroni and cheese,
Dr. Pepper, Skippy peanut butter, and Jolly Ranchers for the
kids. One year I also brought back my skulls.

I had a small skull collection in storage and thought my students in Budapest would enjoy seeing them. I even had a human
skull. Before leaving for Hungary, I wrapped the bones up carefully in my clothes and put them in my carry-on. I didn't want to
risk some baggage handler breaking them.

When I got to the airport, I put my carry-on onto the conveyor belt at the security check. The carry-on rolled through the
X-ray machine. All of a sudden the conveyor belt stopped. The
man looking at the monitor called over another man.

Uh-oh, I thought.

They reversed the conveyor belt and called a third man over.
One of them pointed at the screen. His name tag said "Roberto."

"What do you have in there?" Roberto asked.

"My toothbrush," I answered.

"What else?" he asked.

"Uh . . . toothpaste."

I'd heard stories about airports taking your stuff and feeding
it to the dogs that sniff for drugs. I didn't want Rover gnawing on
any of my bones!

"And what else?" Roberto asked.

"Oh . . . well . . . just some skulls," I said casually.

He looked at me funny.

"I teach science," I said.

"Could you open your bag, please?" he asked.

Just my luck. Never in my life had I been stopped at an airport, and now—the one time I'm carrying a bag full of skulls—they stop me.

I opened it and laid the skulls on the conveyor belt.

"Could you unwrap these, please?" he asked.

Roberto watched carefully as I unwrapped the skulls.

"What's that?" he asked, pointing to one of the skulls.

"This one's a baby crocodile," I said.

I continued unwrapping.

"And this one here is a chimpanzee skull," I said.

Pretty soon I had five skulls laid out on the conveyor belt. And there I was, in the middle of the airport—teaching a science lesson.

Soon I was free to go. I wrapped the skulls back up, waved good-bye to Roberto, and flew to Budapest.

The next summer, before I flew back to the States, I asked my Hungarian friend Imre what I should bring back for my friends.

"Definitely Pick salami," he said. "It's so good that in Hungary, if you're pulled over by the police and have a Pick salami, you can just give him your Pick and you don't have to pay your ticket."

So I bought a half dozen giant Pick salamis, loaded them into my suitcase, and flew back home for the summer.

As I waited at baggage claim back in the States, a scary-looking lady walked up to me.

"Do you have any food?" she asked.

"Just salami," I answered.

Surely that wouldn't be a problem, I thought. When they say "food," they mean fruits and vegetables and stuff that the Mediterranean fruit flies eat.

"Please go over there," she said, pointing to the next line.

I looked over at the line. Everybody was unloading their suitcases.

"Not again!" I cried.

I lugged my bags onto the conveyor belt. The bag moved through the X-ray machine. The belt stopped. The man pointed to the screen. His name tag said "Gilbert."

"Where's Roberto?" I asked.

"Huh?" he said.

"Never mind," I said.

"Could you open your bags, please?" Gilbert asked.

I opened them. The salamis were right on top.

"Salami, huh?" he said. "We'll have to take them."

He began to put on his gloves. I felt like a druglord.

"Why?" I whined.

"Not allowed in the country," he said matter-of-factly.

"But *every* tourist shop in Budapest sells these stupid salamis," I said. "And there isn't one sign anywhere in Hungary that says you can't bring them into the United States. I don't have any other souvenirs for my friends. *Please* don't take them. *Please!* I *beg* you!" (I teach drama too.)

"Sorry, sir. We have to. The law," said Gilbert.

He pointed to the wrapped skulls. "What are these?" he asked.

"Skulls," I answered. "I'm a science teacher."

"Could you please unwrap them?"

I unwrapped the crocodile first.

"Where'd you get this one?" he asked.

"I found it in Brazil."

Next I unwrapped the chimpanzee.

"What about this one?"

"A friend gave it to me," I answered.

Then I unwrapped the human skull.

"And this one," he asked, "what happened to him?"

I looked up at Gilbert.

"He took my salami."

# Saved

*Each year* our town blocks off one of the big streets downtown on the first Saturday in May for the annual Pet Parade. The Pet Parade has been around as long as I can remember. I used to pull my own guinea pigs in my Radio Flyer when I was a kid.

Children from the whole town parade their pets. All animals are allowed, and anything goes. I've seen bunnies pushed in strollers, hamsters pulled in wagons, kittens carried in bicycle baskets, and bird cages pushed on skateboards.

Every pet is covered with bows, every bicycle wheel is woven with crepe paper, and every handlebar is wrapped with streamers. The kids walk with their class behind their school banner. Most of my students participate. I walk with them. Last year I put dog ears on my nephew and gave him a piggyback ride the whole way.

This year, the week before the parade, Sarah sat at her desk whimpering.

"What's wrong, Sarah?" I asked.

She continued to cry. I walked over to her desk and crouched down.

"Sarah, what's wrong?" I asked again.

Through her sniffles, I made out that Barnie had died last

night. Barnie was her rat. Barnie had been in for sharing on Bring Your Pet Day.

"I'm really sorry, honey," I said quietly.

"And . . . and . . . now . . . I . . . can't . . . walk in . . . in . . . the parade," she cried.

Immediately I put on my repairman's hat. What could I do? I had already promised Melanie that she could carry Penel. And I had told Katie that she could walk with one of the hamsters. All the other pets were spoken for as well. Sarah continued to cry.

Then I spotted him. In the reading corner. On the chair.

"What about taking Snoopy?" I suggested.

Snoopy sat on my reading chair by the bookshelf. I bought him at a garage sale my first year of teaching and he has been with me ever since. He is our class mascot. His tail is gone now. His nose was loved off years ago. And these days he's more gray than white, but I'm afraid to put him in the washing machine for fear he'll completely come apart. When he is not in the reading chair, he is in someone's lap—usually during silent reading, sometimes after a wipeout on the blacktop, and always during storytime. But Snoopy is a good sport. He has been pulled on and fought over and sat on for twenty years, but he hasn't left yet.

He'd make a good teacher.

"You know, Sarah, Snoopy's never been to the Pet Parade," I said softly. "All these years he's watched Penel leave and he *never* gets to go. I think he wishes he could. But nobody will take him."

Sarah sniffed twice.

"Of course he might get cold. He'll need a sweater or something. We could make him something at school. He's never been out before, you know. You'd really have to take care of him."

Sarah sniffed again, but only once this time.

"How 'bout it? Would you take Snoopy?" I asked. "Please."

There was a pause. Then she nodded yes. And on Saturday morning, our class marched with seven dogs, four cats, six guinea pigs, three rabbits, two hamsters, three rats, and one well-loved stuffed animal who saved me.

# Where's the Hole Punch?

*Have you ever* observed how kids clean out their desks? They don't take out their books and papers and lay them on top of their desks. Oh no. They reach their arms into the desks, pull everything out at the same time, and spread it all out on the floor like it's their Halloween candy. The room looks like Wal-Mart after an earthquake.

I know it is time to clean out our desks when I can't find any more pencils or Wite-Out or erasers or hole punches, when there is some nasty smell that I cannot identify, or when one of the hamsters is missing again.

Once a month I put on my hardhat, tie red and white plastic tape across my doorway, and lay out orange cones in the hall. I stand guard at the wastebasket, handing back math papers that should have been turned in seven months ago and book reports that forgot where the finished work basket is.

There are certain students you always have to watch closely on desk-cleaning day. This year it is Joshua.

"Joshua, come here!" I shouted after he threw a pile into the garbage.

I handed him back his math book.

I am relieved to know that should there ever be an emergency, we could survive for three months. Today I discovered half a tuna fish sandwich, a black banana, a bag of Cheetos, and two hardboiled eggs. *That* was in Ryan's desk.

Melissa found the remains of a peanut butter and jelly sandwich in a tupperware container. If she entered it in the science fair she could probably win third prize.

I used to dread desk-cleaning day. But then I read *7 Steps for Highly Effective Teachers* and made a paradigm shift.

Now we have desk-cleaning parties and we play lots of games. My favorites are Stuff the Wastebasket Until It Overflows, Stand on the Trash in the Garbage Can to Make It Go Down, and "Oh, There It Is!"

I even hand out prizes. This month Katie won for largest collection. She had thirteen juice boxes in her desk and twenty-seven more in her cubby. Anthony won for most pencil shavings. Erika won for the most sunflower seeds ever brushed onto the floor. And Michael won for most overdue library books discovered (he had already paid for them to be replaced).

Sometimes I wonder why kids who won't clean out their binders, or pick up their jackets off the floor, find desk cleaning so much fun.

Maybe because it is fun to go to the bathroom and wet ten paper towels till they are sopping and wipe out the desk with them and make the inside of the desk sopping wet too.

Maybe because it is fun to squirt the desktop twenty-five times with the spray bottle full of soapy water, then watch the soapy water drip onto the floor, and when the teacher screams to get some paper towels, run to the bathroom, then run back and say there aren't any more.

Maybe because it is fun to watch the teacher put his hand on his forehead and roll his eyes and shake his head when Jenny pulls out seven hole punches from her desk, when just this morning she asked me for one.

# The Talk

*At the end of the year,* the fifth graders get the Big Talk. The girls go to Mrs. Garcia. The boys go to Mr. Clark. The teachers put it off as long as they can.

This May Mr. Clark had to have an emergency appendectomy and was out for two weeks. Cathy came to see me.

"Phil, could you fill in for Ken next week? I'll cover your class," she said.

"No way!" I screamed.

"Please. We need a man," she begged.

"I'm not talking to forty-five fifth grade boys about sex," I shouted.

"You don't have to talk to them about sex," Cathy said. "You just have to talk to them about the changes that will take place in their bodies."

"I can't," I said. "I had most of those boys two years ago. I know them all. They lose it if you say the word *armpit.*"

"Please," she said.

"Give 'em a razor," I said.

"Please," she begged again. "I'll make you dinner."

"Really?" I asked.

"Anything you want," she said.

"Can you make lasagna?" I asked.

"Yep," she said.

I sighed. "OK," I said. "I'll do it."

"Thanks," Cathy said. "I owe ya." And she left.

The next week, after lunch, it was time to separate the boys and the girls.

Dominga walked up to me. I had Dominga two years ago.

"Mr. Done, I don't want to learn about sex from Mrs. Garcia!" she cried. "She'll ruin it."

"Dominga, she's just going to talk with you about growing up. That's all. Now go on."

She walked into Mrs. Garcia's room with her head down. Frankly, I wouldn't want to learn about sex from Mrs. Garcia either.

The boys walked into my room and sat down.

"Hi, boys," I said, "Today we are going to learn about the changes that will take place in your bodies when you get older. Does anyone have any questions?"

Silence.

I scratched my head.

"Well, is there anything that any of you would like to know about the changes that are going to occur as you get a little older?" I asked.

More silence. I looked around the room.

Then I got an idea, and I grabbed some paper and pencils.

"OK, boys," I said, "now I am going to give you each a piece of paper. On it I would like each of you to write down any questions you might have about anything related to the changes in your body. And I expect you all to write something. I will read each question aloud and then we can discuss it. OK?"

"OK," they all said quietly.

I handed out the paper. Immediately everyone began to write. This is great, I thought. We will have lots to discuss. After a couple of minutes, I collected the papers and looked at the first paper.

Scribble.

I looked at the second.

Loopty loops.

I looked at the third.

Garfield.

I glanced through the whole stack.

All scribble but one.

"Well, boys," I said, "only one of you has a question."

They were all quiet.

I read it out loud. "Can we go outside and play basketball?"

They stared at me. No one moved.

I looked around the room. "OK," I said, "let's go."

"Yeah!" they all shouted.

"But," I said, "after we play hoops, go home and put some deodorant on, OK?"

"OK," they all said.

And we went outside.

I wonder if I still get my lasagna.

# New Definitions

*Did you know* that since 1828, over 60,000 new words have been added to the dictionary? And did you also know that there is a whole team of people working for *Webster's New World College Dictionary* who look for new words and write their definitions? They wrote definitions for new words like *aw-shucks* and *roadkill*. When I retire, that's what I want to do. In fact, I have already started collecting new definitions for when I work at Webster's.

**WING** (verb) to walk into your classroom on Monday morning with absolutely no plans and then teach for six straight hours

**PISTOL** (noun) a kid who gets into trouble often and does not follow class rules

**FILLER** (noun) Simon says, hangman, or any other activity you can do the last period on Friday when you are too tired and have forty-five minutes left in the day

**WRINGER** (noun) see *pistol*

**PREP** (noun) a period in which teachers do everything but prepare for the next class; usually involves meeting with colleagues, picking up backpacks, mediating arguments, reviewing the rules about snowball fights, calling parents, or running to the bathroom

**PILL** (noun) see *wringer*

**RECESS** (noun) a fifteen- to twenty-minute block of time in which teachers stand in line to use the copier

**CORKER** (noun) see *pill*

**FAST** (adverb) the speed at which a teacher can unjam the copier at recess

**CARROT** (noun) a video, free time, extra PE, a field trip, Cocoa Puffs, or any other thing that you can use to get a child to do what you want

**PROP** (noun) anything you can hit someone with or drop during the school play

**JOKE** (noun) evaluations by the principal

**BABYSITTING** (noun) the act of watching kids and trying to maintain order on Halloween

**PERFORMANCE** (noun) smiling in front of all the kids and room moms when you open the horseshoe napkin holder that they all chipped in on for your end-of-the-year gift

**SAINT** (noun) first grade teacher

# Class Placements

*At every elementary school* teachers get together with their principals at the end of May or early June and set up the classes for the following year. At our school we write the kids' names on index cards and lay them all out on a table and shuffle the cards around until the classes are balanced. We also divide and conquer.

"Where do we put Ronny next year?" Cathy asked.

"Away from Stephen," I replied.

"And where do we put Stephen?" she asked.

"Away from Brian," I said.

"And where do we put Brian?" she asked.

"Away from all sharpened pencils, compasses, paper clips, rulers, yardsticks, and fire extinguishers!"

There are a lot of factors that go into setting up a class. Teachers look at the balance of boys and girls, ethnicities, and academic levels. And there is something else we consider.

Now, I am sure that I will be fired for divulging what I am about to tell you. But here goes:

Schools honor parent requests.

Yes, it's true. In most schools, the principal will say, "It is the school's policy that we do not honor parent requests for teachers." This simply is not so. The schools say this because they do not want the hassle, they do not want to deal with pushy moms and dads, and they want the parents to believe that all the teachers in the school are equally good.

Some parents write letters to the principal anyway. I have seen them. It's amazing how many squeaky wheels get the teacher they want.

But parents aren't the only ones who make requests. Teachers make requests too. Recently I walked into Marion's room.

"Hi, Marion. I love your outfit. Would you like me to take your yard duty today?" I asked.

"You're early," she said.

"Huh?" I asked. "What do you mean?"

"Well, last year you didn't start buttering me up till the end of May," she said.

I laughed. "I'm not buttering you up."

"Then what's that?" she asked, pointing to the wine bottle in my hands.

I set it on her desk.

"OK, so I am," I said. "But look what good it did me. You still gave me Stephen."

She laughed.

"This year I thought I'd better start early," I said. "What's the name of that kid who is always in Cathy's office whenever I go in there?"

"Juan," she said.

"I think he'd do really well in Dawn's class," I said. "I really think he needs a good motherly influence. And what's the name of that other boy who is always sitting right next to you at all the assemblies?"

"Oscar."

"I think Oscar needs to be in Dawn's class too," I said.

She smiled and said, "I think Oscar needs a positive male role model."

I took back the wine.

# Out of the Mouths of Babes

*Why do they call* the staff room "the lounge"? As if the place were filled with plush chairs, bowls of peanuts, and a guy named Sam playing the piano in the corner.

No matter what school you're in, all staff rooms look the same. The cupboards are full of coffee mugs, the refrigerators are full of Tupperware, and the bulletin board is full of job ads for teaching positions in the Bahamas.

The conversations in staff rooms are always the same too. They begin something like this: "Did you hear what so-and-so said today?" or "Guess what happened in my room this morning," or "I've got one for you!"

On the last week of school Kim, Mike, Dawn, Lisa, and I were sitting in the staff room at lunch sharing our latest stories about the kids. The following are my guess-what-so-and-so-saids for the year:

**ANTHONY:** Mr. Done, if we start learning about weapons, can we watch *Mission Impossible?*

| ME: | What's wrong, Andrew? |
|---|---|
| ANDREW: | (looking worried) Mr. Done, when I go to college, can I take my turtles? |

| ME: | Does anyone know what a vegetarian is? |
|---|---|
| RYAN: | Of course. Someone who doesn't eat hamsters. |

| ME: | Good-bye, Tomoya. |
|---|---|
| TOMOYA: | Good-bye, Teacher! See you yesterday! |

| ME: | Boys and girls, did you know that Mozart died at the age of thirty-seven and Gershwin died in his thirties too? |
|---|---|
| MATTHEW: | I don't want to be a composer. |

| NATALIE: | My mom is *so* gullible! Mr. Done, what does *gullible* mean? |
|---|---|

| ME: | What's wrong, Ji Soo? |
|---|---|
| JI SOO: | I'm sick (coughing). I caught a freezing. |

| MELANIE: | My sister is reading *Little Women.* Do you know how many pages it has? Over a hundred! |
|---|---|

| ME: | Does anyone know who sings "White Christmas"? |
|---|---|
| PATRICK: | Mr. Done, everyone knows that. Bill Cosby. |

**ME:** Melissa, do you know what an adjective is?

**MELISSA:** Uh-huh. Adjectives are dress-up words.

**ME:** Emily, what do you want to be when you grow up?

**EMILY:** When I grow up, I am going to get married and have two girls, then get divorced, then be a limousine driver.

**ME:** Carlos, where are you supposed to hang your jacket?

**CARLOS:** On the hooker.

**KEVIN:** When I grow up, I want to move to China.

**ME:** Why?

**KEVIN:** Because it's the toy capital of the world.

**ME:** What do you mean?

**KEVIN:** On all my toys it says, "Made in China."

**ME:** Yes, Joey?

**JOEY:** Mr. Done, if a meteorite is a comet that lands on the earth, what is a meteor-wrong?

**ME:** Can anyone tell me what the Statue of Liberty is holding?

**BRIAN:** An ice cream cone.

**ME:** (walking down the hall) What are you doing, Erika?

**ERIKA:** I'm mad at my mom, so I'm stepping on all the cracks.

| ME: | Justin, you have a choice. You can get off that beanbag right now, or you can go to Miss Carlson's office. |
| JUSTIN: | Does she have a beanbag? |

| AARON: | Mr. Done, I'm going to turn into a new leaf. |
| ME: | That's *over*, Aaron—turn *over* a new leaf. |

| ME: | What's the opposite of rough? |
| KENNY: | Meow. |
| PETER: | Mr. Done, what's algebra? |
| ME: | Hard math. It looks like this . . . (writing $3x + 2 = 17$ on the board) |
| PETER: | My sister is doing the *x*. She's in high school now. |

| ME: | Joshua, if you do that again, you will have to copy pages in the math book. |
| ME: | (later on) Joshua, what are you doing? |
| JOSHUA: | Copying pages. |
| ME: | But you're not in trouble. |
| JOSHUA: | But I probably will be tomorrow. Can I use them for later? |

| ME: | Can anyone tell me why Magellan is famous? |
| STEPHEN: | That's easy. He circumcised the world. |
| ME: | That's circumnavigated, Stephen. Circum*navigated*. |

# The Dinner Invitation

*At the end of the year* I always get a couple of invitations for dinner from some of my students. And usually I go (it beats Top Ramen). In fact, in my early days of teaching I used to announce that I love to be invited over for dinner and my favorite food is lasagna.

It worked. One year I had lasagna for two straight weeks.

But after my first couple of dinners at my students' houses, I noticed a pattern. It seemed that every dinner was exactly the same. I figured there must be some book out there on what to do when you invite the teacher over, because it was the same routine at each home.

When you arrive at your student's house for dinner, you are always greeted at the door by the mom and the dog. The mom will invite you in and the dog will sniff you. Your student will not be there. Yes, the child you have just spent the entire day with—in fact, the last year with—will not be there. Why? Because she is hiding from you. Eventually she will appear peeking from around the kitchen door, but she will not speak. Her younger sister will be with her. She will not speak either.

But soon their nerves will go away, and your tour begins. First stop: your student's bedroom. On your way, you will walk through the hallway. There you will stop and look at every school photo of every child in the family. You will also see the wedding photos of grandma and grandpa, and mom and dad, and every aunt and uncle on both sides of the family.

Then you will reach the bedroom. The bed will be made and the desk will be tidy because your student has been cleaning her room since she invited you two weeks ago. As you enter the bedroom, your student will run to her bed and shout, "Don't look under there!" The closet door will be covered with artwork from school. As you approach the closet door, she will run to the closet, spread out her arms, and scream, "Don't look in there!" Then she will run to the hamster, take him out of his cage, and ask you if you want to hold him. After you say "No thanks" five times, she will finally put the hamster back into his cage and show you the ribbons and medals hanging on the bulletin board over her desk. One at a time.

Your next stop on the tour is little sister's room. She has also been cleaning up her room for you. She will show you all of her medals and ribbons and certificates and stuffed animals too. If you are lucky, she does not have a hamster.

Next you will be escorted to the living room. There you will listen to your student play the piano. She will play "Für Elise." After the concert she will put on her new black tap shoes and perform five hundred time steps and shuffle ball changes on the entryway tiles. The younger sister will put on her new black tap shoes next and dance for you as well.

Finally it is time for dinner. You will be escorted to the dining room, where you will sit next to your student. The children will have set the table. There will be a tablecloth. Of course supper will be lasagna. You will also have French bread and salad. Your student will have made the salad, which you will say how much you like over and over again throughout the meal. The dessert will be bundt cake.

After dinner you will walk back to the living room to look at photo albums. There will be thirty-seven of them. You will flip through them all. They will show you photos of their birthday parties, first days of school, Halloween costumes, visits to Santa Claus in the mall, and shots of the dog being washed. You will also see three hundred photos of the Grand Canyon and just as many with Mickey Mouse.

Finally you will look at your watch and say it is getting late and you must be going home soon. The mom will wrap some lasagna up for you in aluminum foil to take with you.

This year, I was invited over to Emily's house for dinner. It was exactly the same routine—tour of the bedroom, recital in the living room, dinner, photos, and lasagna for home. The only difference was that Emily had a guinea pig, not a hamster. Just before I left, I asked Emily if she had done any of her homework.

"Not yet," she answered.

I leaned over and winked.

"You don't have to do it," I said. "Thanks again for having me over."

The next day at school, I thanked Emily again in front of the class. Then she announced to everyone that I ate three pieces of lasagna and two huge pieces of cake, that I was afraid to hold her guinea pig, and that her mom says I'm a big eater.

"And," she said, "Mr. Done said I didn't have to do my homework because I invited him over."

By first recess there were seven invitations on my desk. Five were from Ronny.

"Hey, Ronny," I said.

He looked up at me.

"These are all from you."

He grinned and said, "If you come over all five times, I won't have homework for a week."

# I Know

*When someone asks me* if I have any kids, I say I have thirty-two. I mean it too. Teachers are the third parent. Once I read an article by Erma Bombeck that I will never forget. It was entitled "I Know." It was about the wisdom of parents. Here are some things that teachers know:

I know you hated it when I called on you in class and your hand was not raised. I wanted to hear your thoughts.

I know you were nervous standing up in front of the whole class to recite your poem. I wanted you to speak in front of others.

I know you did not like reading *Mat the Rat* with me when the others were reading harder books. Remember, you have just started learning English. You will read harder books someday. I promise.

I know you do not want to repeat the same sentence for me and this time stop at the period. I want you to learn to read.

I know you were upset when I did not help you draw the cat. I wanted it to be your cat—not mine.

I know you were frustrated when I did not tell you how to solve thirty-six divided by seven. I knew you could do it.

I know you were waiting a long time while I stood and talked to Miss Kimmy. I wanted you to be patient.

I know you were frustrated when I didn't call on you and I called on Joshua instead. I know you know what six times nine is, and I was not sure if Joshua did.

I know you were mad at me when I called your mom. You need to eat more than a Snickers for lunch.

I know it is frustrating to read slower than your classmates. I read slowly too.

I know you were upset when I wouldn't let you get a drink of water when you said, "Can I get a drink?" Next time you will say "may."

I know it is not your preference to listen to Mozart and Vivaldi and Beethoven and Tchaikovsky. It is good for your soul.

I know you were not happy that I did not tell you how to spell *impossible*. I wanted you to try.

I know you hated staying in at recess with me today. I wanted to give you time to finish your work.

I know Anthony had his birthday party last night and you had to finish building your Pinewood Derby car for Scouts and you couldn't finish your homework and you hated staying after school. I was following through.

I know you didn't like rewriting your paragraph. I wanted you to do your best.

I know you already wrote *threw* and *said* and *school* for me yesterday and the day before that too. I wanted you to learn how to spell.

I know you did not like it when I asked you what you would write in your web if you were Charlotte. I wanted you to imagine.

I know you couldn't concentrate today and I let you go out and play at recess even though you only did five math problems. I had a dog that died once too.

# Have I Taught Them?

*I know they will forget* how to multiply over the summer, and next year's teacher will show them how to do it all over again. I know they will forget the difference between an adverb and an adjective, how to spell *spaghetti,* and when the Pilgrims sailed to the New World.

But have I taught them that it is better to tell me that they did not do their homework last night than to lie?

Have I taught them that it is better to include someone in a four square game than to tell him he cannot play?

Have I taught them how to work in groups of four when there are only two red markers and everyone wants the red one?

Have I taught them how to say "Good morning" when they pass someone in the hall and "Good-bye" when they leave the room?

Have I taught them that Jefferson could not live without books, and neither can I?

Have I taught them how to think when the answer is not right there in the text?

Have I taught them that imagination really *is* more important than knowledge?

Have I taught them that most of Thomas Edison's experiments did not work the first time either?

Have I taught them the joy of singing every day?

Have I taught them the satisfaction you feel when you do your best?

Have I taught them to laugh, but not at others' mistakes or when someone's name is different from your own?

Have I taught them that learning is lifelong and shown them my French homework?

Have I taught them that it is OK to make mistakes and shown them my French homework?

If I have taught them these things, then I do not care if they forget when the Pilgrims sailed to the New World or how to spell *spaghetti*.

# The Last Day of School

*For weeks* I have been wishing that I could fast-forward to the last day of school. But now that it is the last day, I don't want them to leave.

It's never easy for me to let my little birds go. I know the names of all their pets. I was the first one to sign their casts. I know that Joey's dad is not living at home anymore. I know how much they grew on the wall chart.

We mourned together over cats that did not look before crossing the street. We graduated from wide-ruled to college-ruled paper together. We have become a family.

Parents have eighteen years to get ready to send their kids out of the nest. Teachers only get ten months.

The bulletin boards are empty now. The wire hanging across the ceiling is bare too, except for a couple of clothespins that used to hold their artwork. My desk is covered with gift bags full of coffee and mugs and candy and homemade cards. Jenny knitted me a set of coasters.

After they cleaned out their desks and put everything into their cubbies, we began our party. The kids passed out popcorn and pretzels and snack mix. Mrs. Stewart and Mrs. Turner walked around pouring juice. I sat at my desk and watched them talk and laugh and spill popcorn and pretzels and snack mix on the floor.

Then Mrs. Stewart made an announcement and Melanie brought me a present from the class. Everyone got up and stood around me. They leaned in as I unwrapped it.

"I know what it is," said Stephen.

"Don't tell!" screamed Emily.

"Wow," I said, taking it out of the box. I read the cover. "*Mr. Done's Memory Book*. It's beautiful. When did you make it?"

"When you were absent," said Natalie. "Mrs. Stewart came in and did it."

I pretended to be shocked.

"Why, you sneaky little kids," I said.

They laughed.

I thumbed through the pages.

Anthony had written, "Dear Mr. Done, I will miss you. I liked your funny stories." And he had drawn a picture of me with a giant coffee mug.

"Do I look like that?" I asked.

"Yeah!" they all screamed.

"Thanks a lot."

Tomoya had written, "Dear Mr. Done, thank you for teaching me English. It is much bigger now."

I smiled. "Thank you, Tomoya," I said. "Your English is so good now."

After thanking them all, I asked them to take their seats for the last time. Then, ten minutes before the bell, I began my final speech of the year.

"Boys and girls," I said, "it's been a great year . . ." My voice started to crack. "And now," I continued, "it is time for you to go to fourth grade. You've worked hard. You're ready. Peter, what is eight times seven?"

"Fifty-six!" he shouted.

"Good. Now remember, everyone, be kind to one another. Remember to do your homework. Remember to put your name on your papers. Remember to feed the bunny rabbit. Natalie, how many *e*s in *sincerely?*" I asked.

"Two," she said.

"Good." I took a deep breath and continued, "Now, I want you all to come back and visit your old third grade teacher sometime. Teachers like it when their kids come back to visit. OK?"

"OK," everyone said in unison.

I wiped my eyes.

"OK, troops, let's get ready to go."

Then they all stood up. Without speaking, all thirty-two lined up for hugs. I bit my lip as I tousled hair and patted heads good-bye. Natalie cried. So did Stephen. Emily handed me a coloring book page she had colored last night. Ronny would not let go.

"Now, now, Ronny. You can't miss the bus."

"OK," he said. "Bye, Mr. Done."

"Bye, Tiger."

He let go and ran out the door.

"Hey, Ronny!" I shouted.

He turned around. "Yeah?"

"Don't forget your backpack," I said.

He smiled. "Oh, yeah."

He ran back, grabbed it, and hurried out the door.

When they were all gone, I picked up a juice box from under Katie's desk, loaded my good-bye presents into a shopping bag, took down the world map, and stacked the chairs. Then I erased the "1 Day Left" on the corner of the whiteboard, closed the piano lid, took one last look around the room, turned off the lights, and locked the door.

# About the Author

Phillip Done won the Schwab Foundation Distinguished Teacher Award. Nominated for the Disney Teacher of the Year Award, he has taught elementary school for twenty years. He lives in Mountain View, California.